C000082602

ROMAN
SIEGE WORKS

ROMAN SIEGE WORKS

GWYN DAVIES

TEMPUS

First published 2006

Tempus Publishing Limited
The Mill, Brimscombe Port,
Stroud, Gloucestershire, GL5 2QG
www.tempus-publishing.com

© Gwyn Davies, 2006

The right of Gwyn Davies to be identified as the Author
of this work has been asserted in accordance with the
Copyrights, Designs and Patents Act 1988.

All rights reserved. No part of this book may be reprinted
or reproduced or utilised in any form or by any electronic,
mechanical or other means, now known or hereafter invented,
including photocopying and recording, or in any information
storage or retrieval system, without the permission in writing
from the Publishers.

British Library Cataloguing in Publication Data.
A catalogue record for this book is available from the British Library.

ISBN 0 7524 2897 7

Typesetting and origination by Tempus Publishing Limited
Printed in Great Britain

CONTENTS

ACKNOWLEDGEMENTS

This book stems from the PhD research that I carried out at the Institute of Archaeology, UCL, and I am indebted to my former supervisors, Mark Hassall and John Wilkes, for their rigorous critique of my research methodology and subsequent output. The comments of my examiners, Boris Rankov and Valerie Maxfield, were also very valuable in refining the arguments presented in this text. I have also benefited from the insights and suggestions advanced by my readers Darden Pyron (Florida International University) and Jonathan Roth (San Jose State University). Without Darden's robustly critical stylistic eye and Jonathan's expertise in Roman military affairs, this text would have been much impoverished. I would also like to express my sincerest thanks to my friend Peter Connolly with whom I have shared countless spirited debates over the subject matter of this book and with whom I have had the privilege of conducting fieldwork in both Albania and Italy. The illustrations owe much to the dedication of my former student Robert Carmenate who transformed several unpromising images and produced original artwork in his own right. Finally, I am grateful to the patience and tolerance of Menai Jones. Living with Roman siege works for many long years and enduring treks to remote sites cannot have been easy but her fortitude made this author's task possible.

Gwyn Davies
Florida International University
Miami

INTRODUCTION

Siege operations were an integral element of warfare in the classical world where the reduction of a defended centre may have been necessary for the consolidation of battlefield success, or may have amounted to a formal campaign objective in its own right. Once any decision had been taken to undertake a siege, any subsequent withdrawal before success was achieved (even if carried out for sound tactical reasons) was likely to be portrayed as a defeat. Therefore, if the image of a good and fortunate general was to be sustained, the ancient commander needed a basic competence in the art of siege, and critical to this would have been the choice of the method by which the operation was to proceed. The strength of the defences and the capacity of the besieged to withstand their assailants would have influenced this particular decision, and it should be no surprise that a range of technical aids were developed both to counter any artificial advantage enjoyed by the defenders and to reduce their ability to resist. It is the role of one particular genre of technical assistance, that of 'siege works', that forms the basis of this book.

For the purposes of this argument, the term *siege work* will be taken to encompass all those structures and features *constructed* by an assailant for the purpose of undertaking operations (either directly or indirectly) against a defended centre. As it is the besieger's perspective that will be our focus, the defensive counter-measures to these offensive siege works will not be discussed explicitly.

Furthermore, this definition of siege work excludes any analysis of the *siege train* (that assemblage of engines and machines deployed to assist with the assault) or the various sheds and protective housings that enabled covered approaches to be made to the enemy walls. Along with the artillery, these adjuncts may have played a pivotal role in ensuring the final success of any operation, but their essentially mobile character and the fact that they were assembled rather than constructed, serve to distinguish them from the 'fixed' structural elements that fall within the scope of this book.

Roman approaches to siege warfare and the construction of siege works should not be considered in isolation from developments that took place elsewhere in the ancient world. After all, the Romans were not shy to adopt and adapt alien technologies when they improved their military capacity and there is little doubt that the experiences of others in the prosecution of siege operations would have been studied with considerable interest. If the Romans, therefore, may not have been responsible for inventing any given generic siege work type, it is possible to assert that their elaboration and systematic application of the siege system remained unparalleled until the introduction of powder artillery in the early modern period.

Diodorus Siculus points out that it was from the Greeks that the Romans 'had learned siegecraft and the use of engines of war for demolishing walls' and by being 'pupils who always outstripped their masters' they 'had then forced the cities of their teachers to do their bidding'.[1] Whether or not this testament to Roman adaptibility is strictly correct in ascribing the role of mentors solely to the Greeks, it is clear that the Hellenistic world had been a proving ground for the rapidly evolving science of 'poliorcetics' from the mid-fifth century BC.[2] But as interesting as it would be to provide an account of the historical evolution of siege works, the focus of this book on the Roman world means that we must concentrate on the use and development of these structures in Roman offensive operations. To this end, the different types of siege work are divided between a limited set of categories (e.g. 'circumvallation' or 'mines') each of which receive detailed consideration in separate chapters. For each of the resulting categories of siege work, the argument seeks to establish: the historicity of its use; its physical form and the mode of its construction; the function that it was designed to fulfil; and its overall integration into the chosen tactics of the siege commander.

The main objective of this book is to raise the awareness of the importance of field works to the success (or otherwise) of Roman siege operations. This is particularly important as ever since the publication of technical treatises by classical authors, the significance of siege works has been persistently downplayed in favour of the more glamorous contribution made by siege engines, and it is hoped that the following pages will serve as a corrective to this rather distorted perspective.

1

THE LITERARY SOURCES

We can distinguish between two types of classical texts that make mention of siege operations: those works concerned with the elaboration of a narrative (where a siege may be recorded, in more or less detail, as another episode of history) and those works that profess to serve as technical *aide memoires* for field commanders. Notwithstanding the avowedly practical emphasis of the 'handbooks', the authors responsible for their compilation have very little to say either about the form and composition of siege works or the relationship of these structures to siege strategies. Rather, their main concern lay in discussing the nature and purpose of the siege train and in devising ruses through which the defenders might be deceived. Accordingly, for a more developed impression of the reality behind the conduct of siege operations, it is often better to consult the narrative accounts directly, even if this material is often idiosyncratic or elliptical.

THE NARRATIVE SOURCES

These various narrative texts range from detailed historical writing covering specific campaigns (such as Caesar or Josephus) to sweeping treatments of a much broader temporal spectrum (e.g. Eutropius or Florus). Whereas the latter texts cannot compete with the former in reproducing the minutiae of individual actions, the brevity of their coverage may nonetheless include astute observations deserving of notice. For example, although Caesar[1] remains the most obvious (if partisan) primary source for an account of events at Dyrrachium (48 BC), Florus' reflective questioning of the logic that informed Caesar's campaign ('but what harm could a siege do to an army which, from its command of the sea, could obtain supplies of every kind in abundance?')[2] stands as a trenchant critique of the besieger's methodology, even if the depth of the Caesarian narrative is not included (*colour plate 1*). A further advantage of works that approach history with such a broad brush is that they sometimes mention incidents which would otherwise remain unknown, something particularly valuable for periods when detailed sources are unavailable. Although these citations may relate to minor incidents of little intrinsic interest (such as the siege of Cosa/Compsa in a small-scale uprising in 48 BC),[3] they may also refer to more significant episodes such as Diocletian's siege of Alexandria, AD 297-8, a major undertaking of eight months' duration.[4]

Occupying the middle ground are the more ambitious works of general history by such authors as Polybius, Livy or Dio Cassius, providing seamless narratives to link the great events of the past. These introduce much incidental detail to enhance the unfolding of events, and sieges are often chosen as melodramatic stages upon which momentous incidents can be readily enacted. This temptation to treat siege as a literary *topos* might lead to descriptions being couched in standardized terms and in actions being represented in a formulaic style, with only a passing relevance to the actual course of events. By way of illustration, Valerius Maximus' concern in his compendium of ephemera is to exemplify human emotional behaviour. Sieges mentioned in his text are therefore included to indicate the extremities to which humans will descend in order to survive. Thus, the details that are relayed as to the siege of Calagurris (72 BC) refer to the salting of the dead to allow the defenders to maintain their food supply,[5] whilst the account of Metellus' investment of various Cretan strongholds (68-67 BC) emphasizes the fact that the besieged were forced to drink their own urine and that of their animals.[6]

However misplaced the emphasis in some of these records (at least from our perspective), the focusing of attention on specific siege incidents does mean that some record of events may survive for modern analysis. Of course, the face-value acceptance of the material contained in these sources should always be questioned. Polybius, after all, passes scathing comment upon the accuracy of contemporary historians:

> As for sieges, descriptions of places, and such matters, it would be hard to describe adequately how they work them up for lack of real matter ... (how they) find it necessary to place before their readers all the devices, all the daring strokes, and all the other features of sieges in general, and in addition to this ... adding inventions of their own.[7]

This failure to deal with the material 'on a proper scale' is only one of many potential dangers in adopting an uncritical view of the literary evidence.

It is worth emphasizing that classical authorship produced texts with little claim to impartiality. Narratives were produced for a variety of didactic, promotional and rhetorical purposes and the events that they related and the information that they contained were manipulated to reinforce the central message. Thus, although Caesar provided a thorough recital of the measures undertaken to achieve the reduction of various Gallic *oppida* (57-51 BC), his portrayal of a determined, meticulous and, above all, ruthless commander, was clearly intended for consumption in the domestic political arena. His self-depiction as a forceful leader blessed with fortune and an active servant of the state interest, was calculated to persuade his readers of the justice of his claim to the leadership of the Roman world. In such circumstances, it is not surprising that he seeks to deny responsibility for the rare reverse at Gergovia (52 BC), where the impetuosity of the troops, and not an error of generalship, is given as the reason for the failure.[8]

Besides concealment, a propagandist might also harness exaggeration to serve the cause, as Caesar demonstrates in his Alesian account (*colour plate 2*). Whereas Caesar provides a detailed description of the measures undertaken here to fortify the line of contravallation,[9] modern excavations have allowed these statements to be tested. Although the obstacle field

Towards Alesia

Stimuli

Lilia (8 rows)

Cippi (5 rows)

Rampart and Towers
<< 80 feet >>

1 The obstacle field at Alesia as described by Caesar

provided in front of the contravallation in the vulnerable plaine des Laumes comes closest to approximating the Caesarian account (despite some significant discrepancies as to the configuration of its component elements), other sectors were much less well-defended. This disproves the monolithic character of the works implied by Caesar. Furthermore, his brief statement that he ordered the completion of a further line of circumvallation by way of 'parallel entrenchments of the same kind facing the other way'[10] is clearly inaccurate. Excavations reveal that even on the level ground of the plaine des Laumes, the security zone was much less powerful than that provided for the comparable sector of the contravallation. Despite his account being flawed by propagandist excess (presumably designed to suggest the industry of his troops and the foresight of their commander), Caesar's description (1) does include the various structural elements that were actually deployed at various points around the encirclement. However, these elements have been conflated into a single unified system instead of being recognized as a patchwork of different components employed in various configurations in different sectors. Caesar's report may therefore be considered disingenuous but not entirely inaccurate. The requirement of extensive archaeological intervention to verify the degree to which reality reflects representation should caution against any uncritical acceptance of even the most 'authentic'-sounding ancient source.

Besides propagandists like Caesar, other writers exaggerated their material. Writers of heroic poetry such as Lucan or Silius Italicus naturally introduced some element of hyperbole into their work, but other, more conventionally 'accurate' writers also adopted superlatives or other flourishes in their descriptions. Josephus, for example, informs us that whole forests were stripped and 'enormous masses of stones' were collected by Vespasian to be used in the siege of Iotapata (AD 67).[11] Similarly, Appian refers to the two massive rams deployed by Censorinus at Carthage (149 BC), one of which, he claims, required 6,000 footsoldiers to drive it forward![12] The improbability of this latter statement can be gauged by comparing it with the example of the two huge rams encased within mobile penthouses employed by the renowned Hellenistic city-taker, Demetrius Poliorcetes, at Rhodes (305-304 BC), each of which 'only' required 1,000 for motive power.[13]

Exaggeration, however, may have served a useful function as a device to ensure that what the author thought to be unusual practice received due attention. Accordingly, although it might be interesting to quantify the actual volume of stone brought to Iotapata or to know the exact number of men needed to bring up the ram at Carthage, it is more significant to note the *relative* weight placed upon the incident by the ancient author. It is the divergence from the norm implicit in such action that required particular emphasis. For example, there is Velleius Paterculus' statement that Caesar's 'feats about Alesia were of a kind that a mere man would scarcely venture to undertake, and scarcely anyone but a god could carry through'.[14] Even if we allow for hagiographic excess, this observation nonetheless betrays the sense of awe engendered amongst near contemporary observers by the scale of the Caesarian works around the *oppidum*. Viewed in this light, the language of exaggeration should not, therefore, be dismissed out of hand as the product of a febrile imagination busily 'working up' the material in the Polybian sense; instead, it also serves to alert the modern reader to the occurrence of what were considered to be genuinely exceptional events.

Other examples where historical reality has been distorted for overall effect are not hard to find. For instance, the point has been made that the duration of the siege of Veii was deliberately extended so that 'Roman heroism invited comparison with Greek and a prolonged siege of a redoubtable opponent could not but evoke the 10-year siege of Troy'.[15] Livy refers[16] to the operations of 401-400 as being the third year of the campaign when in fact he should have referred to the fifth year, a 'mistake' that amounts to 'tacit proof that the start (of the war) was pushed back two years to secure a 10-year length'.[17] Somewhat similarly, Livy's account of the fall of Gabii (c.520 BC) has also been viewed as 'entirely imaginary', the events being concocted out of the conflation of two episodes from Greek history and grafted on to the Roman annals 'to provide flesh and blood to an otherwise emaciated fact'.[18]

The phraseology employed by the classical writers can also be problematic, particularly where descriptive devices are deployed for pleasing rhetorical effect or to reflect literary convention. By way of illustration, one observation often resorted to whenever an attacker found himself particularly hard-pressed was that the assailant was 'less besieger than besieged'. This phrase would appear to have made its debut in the Thucydidean account[19] of the discomfort endured by the Athenian expeditionary force engaged in the siege of Pylos (425 BC), but the frequency with which it recurs in later texts suggests its general acceptance as an elegant shorthand tool of convenience. Examples of this formula in its various guises can be found in Plutarch's account of Gn. Cornelius Scipio's investment of Mediolanum (222 BC),[20] in Dio Cassius' summary of Caesar's actions at Avaricum (52 BC)[21] and in versions of the fateful siege of Aquileia (AD 238) by Maximinus given by both Herodian[22] and the compiler of the *Scriptores Historiae Augustae*.[23] In these particular incidents it is only the last episode that may actually reflect reality, with Maximinus' forces being crippled by famine as a result of the speed of their advance, the prior devastation of the city's *territorium* and the senatorial decree withholding the transfer of supplies to the imperial army. The applicability of the phrase in the first two cases is less clear. There is the suspicion that Plutarch exaggerated Scipio's difficulties with the Insubres in order to accentuate the contribution made by his exemplar, Marcellus, and whilst Caesar's account of the operation before Avaricum[24] concedes that the army was initially short of supplies, his prompt demonstration in force allowed it the subsequent freedom to forage at will.

Apart from a commonality of phraseology, certain authors sometimes resort to conventional literary *topoi* in order to enliven their accounts or to pad out otherwise bare narratives. Thus both Orosius and Florus report (presumably via their mutual source) that the defenders of Numantia (134-133 BC), when faced with the inevitability of defeat, chose to commit suicide,[25] whilst Appian's much more comprehensive account merely states that the town was forced to surrender through famine.[26] It seems likely that version of events could be coloured by perceptions of how proud and resolute defenders were expected to respond, presumably with the examples of Xanthus (42 BC)[27] and Masada (AD 73)[28] in mind. As to imaginative detail, there is a strong suspicion that Dionysius of Halicarnassus' presentation of the sieges undertaken by the early Roman state are often fanciful. For example, when recording Lartius' actions before Fidenae

(494 BC), Dionysius has him 'undermining the foundations of the wall, raising mounds, bringing up his engines of war, and continuing the attacks night and day',[29] tasks that a vigorous contemporary commander might be expected to pursue but which are highly improbable in the fifth century BC. Accordingly, details of this nature, tainted by the expectations of a writer producing his work in the early Principate, should probably be considered as secondary embellishment.

This type of anachronism is particularly likely where an author was drawing directly upon verbal tradition, or from some earlier reference work now unavailable for comparison. If Dionysius indulged in solecism he was not alone. For example, in his explanation of the Servian constitution (of c.550 BC), Livy refers to there being two centuries of engineers attached to the 'first-class' (prima) division with specific responsibility for the manufacture and maintenance of siege engines at times of war.[30] This must anticipate future developments as it seems unlikely, at this early juncture, that Roman military organization would be sufficiently advanced to provide for such a corps of specialists. Livy himself makes no mention of sieges being undertaken by the Romans before the abortive attack on Gabii (c.530 BC)[31] and, given the lack of any Roman artillery for another 200 or so years,[32] the relatively simple 'engines' of early siege trains and the limited siege works of that time would hardly have required the establishment of a dedicated engineering contingent.

This tendency to allow anachronism to creep into the text is best illustrated in the speech that Livy ascribes to Appius Claudius (c.403 BC) in describing the situation at Veii: 'the town is hemmed in with vast siege works which confine the enemy within his walls'.[33] This impression is reinforced by subsequent elaboration:

> The rampart and the trench, each involving prodigious toil, they have carried all that distance; forts they erected only a few at first, but since then, with the growth of the army, they have built very many; they have thrown up earthworks, not only against the city, but also facing Etruria, if any aid should come from that side.[34]

This description is more likely to reflect Livy's understanding of contemporary siege operations rather than those conducted some 400 years earlier. The allusion to extensive earthworks strengthened with forts and turrets to counter both internal and external threats, seemingly mirror Caesarian experiences in Gaul. Indeed, had such a system of double investment been put in place, it would be difficult to see how the Veientes could have continued their resistance until 396 BC when Camillus administered his final *coup de grâce*. Rather than attempting the hermetic sealing of a large city, the Roman strategy would have been to establish a number of blockade camps giving the army a degree of protection and allowing enemy movement to be interdicted at will.[35] It is possible that some of these camps may have been linked by entrenchments, thus explaining Livy's reference[36] to a 'double' fortification to resist both sallies and relief efforts from other Etrurian centres.

Apart from the introduction of anachronistic material, some of our sources also create difficulty by their use of inaccurate or insufficiently precise terminology. This can include simple statements that a commander 'besieged' such and such a place without any further supporting information (e.g. the siege of Ercte, c.252 BC, which, despite the commitment of over 40,000 Roman troops, receives only the barest mention).[37] On occasion, the details given of operational procedures fail to allow the particular siege work elements to be identified with any confidence. For example, Livy's relatively detailed account[38] of Scipio's attack on the city of the Ausetani (218 BC) does not clarify whether the blockade was enforced through encampment or circumvallation. Confusion can also result from an author's inconsistent use of terminology. Thus Valerius Maximus uses the word 'agger' in both its meanings as a 'rampart' (in respect of the hastily improvised palisade line of corpses and their equipment, piled around Munda, 45 BC)[39] and as a 'mound/ramp' (as at Lipara, 252 BC).[40] Conventional usage in siege contexts however, generally reserves the word for describing mounds or ramps.

Just as rhetorical flourishes or careless terminology can cause distortion in the texts, so too might the tendency for authors to 'improve' their narratives by the inclusion of spurious anecdotal matter. Although detecting the inclusion of such details may not be too difficult, assessing the degree to which it can be considered as a contrivance can be much more problematic. A good example can be seen in Zosimus' account of how the 'brigand' leader Lydius met his death during the siege of Cremna (AD 277-278). According to Zosimus,[41] Lydius was targeted by a sharpshooting artilleryman as he surveyed the Roman positions through an embrasure in the town wall, the sniper having pre-positioned his catapult behind a concealing screen of infantry (colour plate 3). There would be little grounds for doubting this report (save, perhaps, to query the idiosyncratic prominence attributed to it) had the author not made previous reference[42] to events of a similar nature that took place during Aurelian's investment of Palmyra (AD 272). In this instance, a leading Palmyrene, who indulged in a daily ritual of abusing the emperor from the enemy parapets, was killed by a Persian archer who had been set as a sniper behind a covering body of soldiers. Such an inherently improbable congruence of events only six years apart, suggests that Zosimus may have been tempted to use what may have been a genuine episode to provide a dramatic finale for two separate sieges.

As a further caveat, much of the corpus of surviving classical texts has passed through the filter of copyists and glossators whose various redactions may have diluted the accuracy of the original observations. This may account for the statement in Appian's account of the siege of Dyrrachium (48 BC) where he claims[43] that the Caesarian circumvallation stretched for a distance of 1,200 stades, an error which is likely to reflect corrupt transmission. However, some mistakes should be attributed to the authors themselves. For example, when discussing events at Gergovia, Florus claims that Caesar surrounded the oppidum with 'a rampart, a palisade and a trench into which he admitted water from the river, and also 18 forts and a huge breastwork'.[44] This statement demonstrates a confusion in the locus of events, as these elaborate measures are far more reminiscent of the siege works deployed around Alesia (52 BC) than the double blockade camp actually employed at Gergovia.

Despite the possibility of bias, distortion and error in the narrative sources, these accounts remain invaluable, particularly when this corpus of evidence is compared with the limited information that can be extracted from the avowedly practical 'handbooks' or field manuals that are treated next.

THE TECHNICAL TREATISES

The origin of these manuals lie in the writings of Hellenistic authors such as Polyaenus and Philo of Byzantium, although the (earlier) work of Sun Tzu serves to remind us that the tradition of compiling procedural guidance notes for field commanders was not unique to the classical world. However, given that the works that fall within this category were written with didactic objectives in mind, they actually contain little by way of instruction as to the form and purpose of siege works. The compendium of 'useful' information that they purport to provide, often demonstrated by the use of precedent, is largely restricted. Firstly, we are given technical advice as to engine construction via 'engineering' manuals such as those of Athenaeus Mechanicus or Apollodorus of Damascus (the latter's 'letter' to the emperor explicitly stating his concern to discuss those engines useful for seizing towns).[45] Secondly, there are attempts to coin exemplary strategic aphorisms based on anecdotal evidence, and to translate specific *ruses de guerre* into general principles of siegecraft. Accordingly, any student of warfare who consulted these texts with a view to deciding upon the appropriate methodology of reduction in any given circumstance, or for advice on building siege works, was liable to be disappointed.

In Polyaenus' *Stratagems of War*, it is Greek experience, naturally enough, that is emphasized, although references to foreign enemies (e.g. the Romans at Ambracia, 189 BC, or Cyrus II at Babylon, 539 BC)[46] do give the work a more general application. Polyaenus' aphorisms are intended to provide exempla of good generalship, but their relevance to offensive siege operations are somewhat limited. Apart from outlining what the Athenian commander, Timotheus, believed to be the tenets of successful siege actions (mostly concerned with limiting the degree to which hostile territory was ravaged),[47] the author offers a few individual case studies to illustrate particular points. Perhaps the most interesting of Polyaenus' specimens concern the third-century BC siege of Prinassus by Philip, the son of Demetrius, and the Amphictyonic investment (date?) of Cirrha.[48] The first of these relates how the besiegers, prevented from undermining the walls because of the hard base rock, simulated the continuance of their tunnelling by carrying earth each night from a ravine some distance away, and dumping it in front of their screened mine entrance.[49] When a large mound had been accumulated, the defenders surrendered, believing themselves thoroughly undermined. The second case describes[50] how the assailants discovered a hidden pipe carrying water into the besieged town, but instead of cutting this (as would have been normal practice), they introduced 'a great quantity of hellebore' into the supply and when the defenders became violently ill, the town was taken without further opposition.

Philo of Byzantium, writing in the 240s BC for the Ptolemaic army,[51] offered a more deliberate and systematic treatment of aggressive siege operations by devoting the entirety of his fourth chapter to the subject. In many respects, this text can be regarded as the epitome of scholarship on the matter with only Vegetius' much later work approaching the diversity and depth of Philo's analysis. Notwithstanding this concentration on offensive techniques, Philo gives relatively little advice as to actual methods of siege work construction although he does explore some of the reasoning that lies behind the provision of such structures. Thus it is interesting to note that if the assailant fails to seize the city outright by a sudden *coup de main*, Philo indicates that field fortification should immediately be undertaken. This should take the form of a continuous stockade running from sea to sea (if the target is situated on the coast)[52] or a stockaded camp set 'out of range on the safest ground'.[53] In other words, unless the centre under attack could be isolated with relatively limited effort, this doctrine recommends the establishment of a blockade camp and not a work of circumvallation. Thereafter, Philo suggests[54] that water supplies to the target should be cut or, if a river runs nearby, its course diverted against the enemy walls, a task that he helpfully suggests should be effected by the excavation of 'channels'![55] In a similar vein, his observation[56] that it may be necessary to dig secret tunnels under walls 'in precisely the manner in which miners (of ore) now employ', can hardly be considered informative. This lack of explanation as to either the purpose or methods of mining, can be contrasted with the details that are lavished on the appropriate ways to remove/cross obstacle fields[57] or the tactics of deployment for mobile towers.[58] Significantly, although advice is given[59] as to how to fill in enemy ditches to allow the approach of the engines, ramp/mound construction is not mentioned. This may well reflect the relative scarcity of such structures in Greek contexts[60] but, if Philo's intended readership was to be the officer corps of the Ptolemaic army, then some knowledge of how to approach the *tel* cities so common to their likely theatre of operations, would surely have been advantageous.

Later technical writers continue this reluctance to discuss the methodology of, or reasoning behind, siege work construction. Accordingly, apart from a brief sentence referring to the siege mound at Massilia (49 BC) being raised by cutting down trees and laying them on top of each other,[61] Vitruvius has nothing further to say in the matter, his main concern being limited to the discussion of engines.[62] Frontinus specifically excludes any consideration of either siege works or siege engines alleging 'the invention of which has long since reached its limit, and … the improvement of which I see no further hope in the applied arts'.[63] Instead, he relates how various tactical ruses were employed in the past to bring sieges to a close, in the hope that modern commanders might profit from these experiences. Apart from a short chapter[64] concerning the diversion of streams and the contamination of water supplies, he offers little of relevance.

The works of Onasander and Vegetius, which both offer advice as to 'best practice' for field commanders, do make some limited references to the form and function of siege works. The former, writing in the first century AD, recognizes that sieges demand not only bravery on behalf of the soldiery and the provision of the appropriate engines, but also an understanding of 'military science' by the commanding officer.[65] Thus prudent generals should take steps to ensure that their camps are properly fortified with ditches and palisades[66] and are properly guarded with picquets posted before the town gates to warn of any sudden sortie.[67] Further practical guidance then follows as to the tactics to be used in deploying siege engines and in the timing of assaults by various divisions of the army.[68] There is no attempt to specify which engines should be used in any given circumstance as this is a decision that the commander should make on the spot, based upon his assessment of the available opportunities. Onasander also observes[69] that one of the criteria in making this decision was the relative degree of competence displayed by the workmen charged with the responsibility of manufacturing (or assembling ?) the engines in question. Not only does this suggest the importance of on-site fabrication, but it also discounts the existence of any specialist engineering unit attached to the army which might otherwise have been expected to provide a consistently competent level of service.

Vegetius' text attempts a more thorough review of the tactics and ruses appropriate to siege actions, with nearly two-thirds of his fourth book being devoted to the topic. In the main, this consists either of recommendations as to how the besieged might improve their defences or advice to the besiegers on the engines and related *équipage* useful to the prosecution of operations. Siege works only merit three brief references, a weakness that presumably reflects the limitations of the original source material employed by Vegetius. The first of these is a short allusion made to the siege mound (*agger*), which is simply described as being an earth and timber construction placed 'against the wall' from which 'missiles are shot'.[70] This terse explanation can be contrasted with the details that are given in the same chapter as to the form and purpose of standard items of siege paraphernalia such as penthouses, screens and mantlets, all of which required considerably less sophisticated planning and manufacture. This diffidence reveals Vegetius' superficial acquaintance with the subject: there is no acknowledgement as to the use of alternative construction materials nor of the relevance of other functional roles that such structures may have fulfilled (particularly their employment as assault ramps). Furthermore, the careless statement that the mound was built against the wall, is also misleading: direct contact with the enemy circuit was to be avoided at all times.[71]

Vegetius is a little more forthcoming in his consideration of mining techniques and he outlines the two different objectives that such works might attain.[72] Driving a gallery beneath the defences could either obtain surreptitious entry for a small body of troops or undermine the enceinte. He tells us that the latter aim is achievable by excavating a tunnel under the wall, the foundations of which are then removed and replaced by dry timber props. Once the work is completed, the gallery is filled with brushwood and other inflammable tinder. On firing, the resulting blaze consumes the temporary pile supports and causes the collapse of the wall. Despite this relative wealth of information, Vegetius provides no suggestions as to the manner in which mines should be constructed, nor any advice on how to distract the defenders' attention from the work in progress.

Finally, Vegetius briefly mentions the measures that should be undertaken to prevent besiegers from being taken by surprise in a sudden sally. Against such eventualities, besiegers are recommended[73] to dig a ditch beyond the range of enemy missile fire and to equip the same with a rampart, stockade and small turrets, the whole ensemble being termed a breastwork.[74] That he does not necessarily mean a circumvallation (rather the point of defence of a particular camp or important position?) is perhaps indicated by his subsequent comment that 'often in descriptions of sieges in historical works one finds that a city has been surrounded with a breastwork'.[75] Although ambiguous, this observation would seem to imply that the provision of a comprehensive circumvallation was anachronistic and that such tactics were no longer employed at the time of the writing of the text at the close of the fourth century AD.

AUTHORSHIP, TRADITION AND KNOWLEDGE

It should be emphasized that this separation between the 'narrative' and the 'technical' sources is a distinction of convenience. Even if the manner in which information is presented to the reader may differ radically, the authors shared the same broad classical tradition of 'ethical historiography'[76] in which didactic moral points (dressed up with varying degrees of rhetorical gloss) were more important than the bare 'facts' of history. The provision of *exempla* might not be adequately served by a direct transmission of the course of events, and undue prominence might therefore be ascribed to less salient episodes in order that the audience's attention could be directed towards the underlying message. This form of manipulation is also accentuated by the fragmentary nature of the ancient texts, so that the material included in the later summaries that provide our only evidence for the original work may focus more upon the interests and concerns of the excerptor rather than those of the actual author.[77]

We have already noted how sieges as set-piece actions could be readily exploited for dramatic potential, where the insertion of stereotypical 'incidents' (such as the fanatical resistance offered by Roman deserters at Rhegium, 270 BC, or Syracuse, 212 BC)[78] not only enlivened accounts, but also provided a ready device for conveying the author's didactic purpose. Two such *topoi*, frequently encountered in the description of sieges, may serve to demonstrate the point. The first of these refers to acts of humanity by the besieging commander sufficient to prompt the surrender of the defenders. Thus, Camillus' honourable conduct at Falerii (394 BC)[79] in declining to take advantage of the hostages provided by a treacherous school teacher, or Caecilius Metellus' order to cease firing when the defenders of Centobriga (142 BC?) used their children as a 'human shield',[80] were rewarded by the capitulation of the enemy. This trumpeting of *clementia* not only provided proof of Roman moral superiority, but for authors living in a new age of imperial peace, such an emphasis might also have counterbalanced the savagery of recent civil wars. The second *topos,* concerns the mass suicide of defenders in anticipation of the imminent fall of their city. An interesting study[81] demonstrates the popularity of this particular literary motif in classical literature with most authors professing admiration for the 'nobility', 'resolve' and 'virtue' of those who preferred death over enslavement. However, the Livian accounts of the fall of Astapa (206 BC) and of Abydus (200 BC) condemn the self-inflicted massacres, the act of butchering one's own women and children being likened to the insensate fury of wild animals and a symptom of unrestrained madness.[82] Perhaps intemperate conduct of this nature was regarded by Livy as the antithesis of the Roman ideal of the family, so that outrageous behaviour by the *paterfamilias* might be interpreted as a violation of the most basic moral and social precepts. Josephus' ambivalent version of the suicide of the *Sicarii* at Masada also suggests that the adoption of this appropriately dramatic conclusion to the narrative was tempered by his consciousness of the opprobrium that this form of murder should evoke. Of course, this subtle interaction would have suited Josephus' purpose both as a story-teller and as a polemicist arguing for the futility of Jewish resistance.

Apart from being captives of their own literary traditions, classical writers were also constrained by the nature and extent of their source material. Although it must be assumed that no longer extant works were available for consultation by their later colleagues, modern scholars can only make speculative attempts to reconstruct the contents of these earlier histories. The resulting *Quellenforschung* can be useful in gauging the relative accuracy of any given source, or in establishing the compositional school or narrational genre that is being emulated, but can only hint at the actual information contained in the lost books. A further difficulty of ancient scholarship was the relative paucity of accurate documentary records. This was particularly true for the later empire when 'much imperial history ... took place behind closed doors and was shrouded in mystery.'[83] If facts were hard to ascertain then invention or guesswork may have taken their place. Whilst the resulting *inventio* may have appeared a legitimate tool for the exploration of the past, the interpolation of the author's own interpretations, usually expressed rhetorically, offers the very real danger of the introduction of anachronistic material. The use of eyewitness accounts may have alleviated this problem, but the value of such reports depended upon the accuracy, recall and experience of the witness and the ability of the historian to conduct a proper interview. Polybius was well aware of the inherent pitfalls of this approach: 'For how is it possible to examine a person properly about a battle, a siege or a sea fight, or to understand the details of his narrative, if one has no clear idea about these matters? For the inquirer contributes to the narrative as much as his informant, since the suggestions of the person who follows the narrative guides the memory of the narrator to each incident'.[84] Perhaps the process of site visits that Polybius undertook helped him to phrase his questions to his eyewitnesses in an appropriate manner.

This caveat as to the reliability of witness statements is even more relevant in those cases where the historian cites his own observations as a primary source. In such cases, the question as to whether that individual was in a position to understand the events that took place (either in terms of military experience or of his physical location on the battlefield), is crucial to the degree of authority that should be attributed to his account. In this respect, we might expect to place the greatest weight on the narratives of experienced commanders such as Caesar or Frontinus (whose knowledge of campaigning would have embraced both strategic and tactical matters), whilst distinguished officers such as Velleius Paterculus would have had their own military backgrounds to recommend them. Unfortunately, such logic may not necessarily reflect reality. For example, the heterogeneous authorship of the corpus of texts attributed to Caesar results in a marked disparity between the treatment of the Gallic and Civil Wars (substantially Caesarian in origin) with the later campaigns. It is clear that whoever was responsible for compiling the account of the Spanish War in particular, was only of relatively junior rank, whose focus on small-scale actions and confused summaries of campaign objectives, betray the narrow perspective of the serving field officer. This contrast with the assured handling of strategic issues in the earlier works ensures that the reader must be cautious in accepting the stated interpretations of motivation and policy that inspired the overall course of these campaigns.

Ammianus Marcellinus was another writer with direct military experience, although his perspective (in contrast to the author of the Spanish War) was that of a staff officer. His presence at Amida (AD 359) provides us with a valuable insight into the rigours of standing siege against a well-equipped enemy, and his participation in Julian's Persian campaign of AD 363 gives us the most detailed account of offensive siege operations since Josephus' account of the Jewish War. However, Ammianus' 'desire to entertain as well as to enlighten' make his reports 'a curious blend of colourful generalizations and precise facts ... Machines roar, missiles fly, soldiers struggle and fall; but the result of this conflict is not immediately clear'.[85] Accordingly, the course of events resemble a series of vignettes where the foreground is sharpened at the expense of the background so that details such as the names of the first three men to emerge from the mine at Maiozamalcha (AD 363) are recorded,[86] whilst the nature and method of construction of the 'mound' raised against the same city are not explained. Indeed, siege works in general receive short shrift at Ammianus' hands, although he is happy to provide a short digression outlining the role and method of construction of various siege engines.[87] Although this may reflect siege warfare in the later empire, where the tactics of assault had come to be preferred to the more methodical approaches of the past, it is just as likely that Ammianus had been seduced into discussing engines rather than siege works because the pre-existing literary corpus was similarly biased towards the description of 'machines'.

For a further insight into the reliability of 'eyewitness' testimony by authors themselves, it is worth taking a slightly more detailed look at Josephus' treatment of the Jewish War.

Josephus himself makes the confident claim that 'I wrote my history of the war being a participant in many of the events, and an eyewitness to most of them, I was ignorant of nothing that was either said or done'.[88] Thus, as Josephus offers himself as a primary source, it is legitimate to query the relative accuracy of his observations (or, at least, his memory of them). Although much has been written with regard to his credibility in general,[89] it is the specific detail contained in Josephus' description of sieges that is relevant here. Certainly, his passages provide us with graphic accounts of the Roman army's siege procedures but, at times, the narrative occasions some confusion. An example occurs following the staff conference that rejected the option of a passive blockade of Jerusalem[90] despite which Titus decided to surround the city immediately thereafter with a work of circumvallation to allow hunger to enfeeble the defenders.[91] Josephus seems to draw a casuistic distinction between this work of containment and a 'passive' blockade on the basis that, at some future time, Titus fully intended to revert to direct approaches. This explanation sits uneasily with the various objections that were raised to the mounting of a formal encirclement, as the resulting circumvallation was completed notwithstanding the size of the city, the difficult terrain and the shortage of raw materials (all reasons cited for rejecting the blockade in the first instance). This confusion may lie in Josephus' desire to conceal the impression that Titus had vacillated following the defeat of his first attempt against the Antonia. By calling a staff conference, Titus may have sought to transfer the responsibility for any future setback to his advisers, although his prompt rejection of the *consilium*, may suggest that the commander had been too shaken by his failure to listen to further offensive proposals.

Apart from such ambiguity (whether or not directly intended), Josephus is often very specific in his statements, and although these may appear to be superficially convincing, Broshi has indicated[92] that he was not shy of exaggeration where it suited his purpose. If, therefore, Josephus could be guilty of dramatically overstating the population of

2 The assault
ramp at Masada

Galilee,[93] does this necessarily invalidate his reporting of other information of a similarly precise nature? Apparently not, as Broshi again suggests,[94] Josephus does provide plausible figures as to the strength of the various factions within the walls of Jerusalem, and independent judgements as to his relative accuracy must therefore be made on each individual occasion. Insofar as he relates the dimension of siege works, Josephus is certainly guilty of exaggeration. The assault ramp at Masada (2), supposedly raised as a solid bank over a vertical interval of 200 cubits (100m),[95] in fact spans a vertical interval of 74m,[96] most of which was taken up by the natural spur on which the mound was built (with Lammerer suggesting an artificial fill only 25-30m in height).[97] Whether Josephus was present at Masada or was working from the military commentaries of Flavius Silva, his overestimation of the build up of the ramp by a factor in excess of c.200 per cent, gives general grounds for concern.

To take another example, it seems that Josephus did not witness the siege of Machaerus (AD 72) either, as he reports[98] Lucilius Bassus' initiative in attacking the fortress by throwing a ramp across the 'eastern' ravine. The remains of the *agger* that are apparent today (3), lie on the *western* side of the target and, despite claims[99] for the existence of a second ramp on the eastern flank, it is inherently unlikely that the Romans would have attempted a further approach from this direction. At the very least, Josephus' lack of care in relating the local topography to the line of attack must sound another cautionary note as to his overall reliability.

Despite their inherent flaws and the varying competence of their authors, the written sources remain valuable assets, and their cautious employment allows valuable information to be extracted as to siege operations even if these may not apply to the incident actually being narrated at the time! By way of illustration, Livy's importation of anachronistic material into Appius Claudius' speech may not help us with our understanding of the true situation at Veii, but it does provide an idea of what measures might have been applied by an assiduous siege commander faced with a difficult enemy in a scenario contemporary with the time of writing. Of course, in ideal circumstances, the testimony of the classical author may be tested against excavated data, adding a further dimension to the resulting analysis. Had Caesar not made extensive reference to the different types of anti-personnel devices employed in his obstacle field at Alesia, then it is unlikely that the slight traces of the *cippi* and *stimuli* recovered in the course of modern excavations at the site[100] would have been recognized for what they are (or rather, for what they might be). Furthermore, the very fact that a reference exists for an ancient siege action may be sufficient to trigger further investigation on the ground, as was the case at Cremna.[101]

3 The assault ramp at Machaerus

That the classical texts form a valuable resource for the student of Roman siege warfare cannot be doubted, and although the information transmitted by the same may often be partial and tainted by inaccuracy, it nonetheless allows a modern observer to have some insight into the methods of reduction employed and the motivation underpinning the decision-making of the siege commander. However, given the potential dangers inherent in any uncritical acceptance of these sources, it is important that the reader remains alert to the idiosyncrasies of individual authors whose own agendas may have distorted the strict authenticity of the narrated events and incidents.

2

THE SIEGE IN THE CONTEXT OF ROMAN WARFARE

Before considering the component elements of the siege system it is necessary to discuss sieges within their overall Roman military context. This chapter will indicate briefly how different sets of military, political and topographic factors may have influenced the manner in which operations were prosecuted, and how expectations that existed at the outset of any given campaign may already have determined the chosen methodological approach.

Sieges have comprised an integral element of warfare down to the modern day, where the prevalence of rapid 'fire and movement' doctrines has not completely removed the need for occasional fixed-base operations to reduce particular centres of resistance (e.g. Dien Bien Phu, 1954; Abadan, 1980-81). Notwithstanding such examples, the significance of sieges in the pre-mechanized age was even greater, when the determined defence of key positions could smother offensives by forcing the assailant to waste an entire campaigning season tied down before one or more stubborn target. It is hardly surprising that the Romans should have developed an effective siege capability which allowed their armies to consolidate success in the field by reducing strongholds that otherwise may have presented their enemies with the opportunity to re-group at leisure. However, it cannot be assumed that all Roman armies had an equal capacity to mount sieges as some formations (such as Trajan's force before Hatra, c.AD 117) were clearly under-equipped[1] for any serious attempt at investment. Accordingly, it is likely that the relevant level of operational capability would have depended upon the degree to which sieges could be predicted as a significant feature of any given campaign. Equally, it may also be possible that the perceived importance of any given siege operation can be assessed by reference to the relative effort devoted to its prosecution (in the Trajanic example above, the Emperor clearly realized that his army was disadvantaged and withdrew before serious losses were incurred).

THE 'PLANNED' SIEGE

It would not have been difficult for Roman commanders to anticipate which of their offensive expeditions had the potential to involve complex siege operations, even given the limitations of the intelligence-gathering services at their disposal.[2] For example, the prospect of aggressive action directed against Carthaginian colonies in Sicily or to counter Macedonian/Antiochene expansion in mainland Greece, would clearly entail the reduction of heavily fortified centres held by large and proficient garrisons. Under such circumstances, campaigns could not have achieved any lasting success unless adequate provision had been made for the exigencies of siege warfare. That the Romans were aware of this fact is apparent from such episodes as the siege of Eretria (198 BC), when the combined Roman-Rhodian-Pergamene fleet descended upon the Euboean city and landed troops to press home the attack. Such a venture could only be sustained because the fleet had been generously supplied with artillery and 'other devices' for destroying cities and had embarked sufficient engineers to manufacture new engines from the amply wooded countryside surrounding the target.[3]

This degree of preparedness can also be identified during the opening moves to suppress the First Jewish Revolt. Although he mishandled the operation completely, Cestius Gallus had provided himself with sufficient artillery before marching on Jerusalem (AD 66) because his troops were able to commence sapping the north wall of the Temple precinct after heavy covering fire had cleared the enemy from their parapets. The later statement by Josephus[4] that the Jews defending Jerusalem against Titus had access to 340 artillery pieces, a large proportion of which had been seized in the shameful rout at Beth-Horon, also implies that Cestius' force had been liberally equipped (even though he only had one full-strength legion and up to three legionary vexillations at his disposal).[5] Similarly, Vespasian was under no illusions that his campaign would be any the easier as it seems that his first concern was to concentrate his forces at Ptolemais and to await the arrival of his siege train before he undertook any active measures against Iotapata (AD 67).[6]

One campaign above all demonstrates the value of the planned operation, namely Scipio Africanus the Younger's attack against Numantia (134-133 BC). There can be little doubt that the failures of successive Roman generals to achieve the capitulation of this single hill town of the Arevaci had caused much consternation in the Senate, and Scipio's appointment was a measure of this frustration. Unwilling to jeopardize the reputation won by his seizure of Carthage, Scipio took his 4,000-strong 'troop of friends' (φιλων) with him to Spain,[7] presumably to stiffen the army already in the province which 'was full of idleness, discord and luxury' and 'demoralized by defeat'.[8] Faced with the rigours of an operation in difficult terrain against a determined enemy, Scipio instituted a series of disciplinary measures to improve the fighting quality of his troops. He expelled 'all traders and harlots ... soothsayers and diviners' from his camp, disposed of all superfluous items from the army commissariat and restricted his men's diet to the simplest of foods.[9] Thereafter, he initiated an intensive training regime involving forced marches in strict formation and 'daily fortified new camps one after another, and then demolished them, dug deep trenches and filled them up again, constructed high walls and overthrew them'.[10] This repetitive sequence would ensure that his troops were thoroughly familiar with field fortification techniques. These exercises demonstrate that Scipio had already decided that the most suitable strategy for the reduction of Numantia would be one of containment (*colour plate 4*), and the emphasis that he placed upon the completion of these manoeuvres within a tightly defined time-frame, indicates his concern that his construction parties should be exposed to dangerous enemy sorties for as short a period as possible.

As a further product of this cautious approach, when Scipio was satisfied that he had improved both the discipline and competence of his troops, he ordered that each man should carry a 30-day corn ration as well as seven stakes for building purposes.[11] This latter provision is particularly interesting (even if seven stakes for each individual, rather than the conventional two,[12] may seem a particularly heavy burden), as it implies that Scipio had already been informed of the bleak, limestone hillsides that surrounded the target and the likely difficulty in scavenging sufficient timber for his intended works. Such intelligence as to the nature of the terrain would have been easily obtained from officers who had served under previous consular commands, and that Scipio had noted such briefings is further indicated by the cautious manner in which he advanced towards Numantia (the careful demonstration in force made against the Vaccaei and the Pallantians deterring them from assisting their neighbour).[13]

While the Numantine episode may provide us with our most detailed example of advanced planning for any given siege campaign, there is every reason to suppose that other operations (whether directed against a specific centre or a wider range of targets) would also have involved comparable levels of pre-planning. The prominence that Numantia is ascribed in our sources and the scale of the measures taken to ensure its reduction, bear little comparison to the actual strategic value of the resulting territorial gain. Numantia's seizure was viewed as a political victory and its fate was to serve as a testament to the remorseless nature of Roman hegemony.

This political dimension was also evident during the Roman intervention against Antiochus III and his Aetolian allies, when Acilius' determined (if ponderous) campaign of 191 BC was devoted to the investment of Heraclea and Naupactus. These operations were clearly conducted in a methodical manner, with the consul reconnoitring the former site before establishing an elaborate command structure, with three deputies being assigned a different sector to attack and a fourth seemingly being given the task of co-ordinating matters as a whole.[14] However, with Philip of Macedon (Rome's ally of convenience) attaching whole swathes of enemy territory to himself, this deliberate approach found little favour with Ti. Quinctius Flamininus who berated the consul for wasting the campaigning season on the reduction of only two cities.[15] When the war re-commenced in 190 BC, Acilius was stung into activity by this harsh judgment (Heraclea and Naupactus had, after all, formed the epicentre of the Aetolian opposition), as he seized Lamia (a town that had withstood Macedonian siege in the previous year) after only the barest possible delay and then quickly moved against Amphissa. However, although his actions may have been galvanized by the criticism of his peer, it is clear that Acilius was still intent upon waging 'city-war', and whilst the issue might sometimes be resolved by a sudden assault, the strong likelihood of prolonged siege operations must always have been factored into the campaign planning process.

THE 'REACTIVE' OR 'ENCOUNTER' SIEGE

Sieges that may be considered as falling into this category were those mounted outside the scope of specifically planned operations, where the reduction of a particular centre was not the fundamental objective of the assailant. Instead, such sieges may have come about in response to developments that occurred in the course of a campaign, where events on the battlefield, or manoeuvring by the enemy, prompted the aggressor to undertake investment as an appropriate counter-measure. The less predictable nature of such operations would mean that a commander had less opportunity to prepare a siege train or to secure the necessary supplies for long-term action, and the experience of his troops allied to his own competence would have acquired still greater significance in determining the success of the venture.

In general terms, it is likely that the 'encounter' siege would have taken place in campaigns waged against the less organized polities and tribal states of temperate Europe, as in such areas there would have been fewer heavily defended centres that would have been worth designating as military objectives in their own right. This is not to say that sieges were uncommon in these areas, as it is clear that the pacification of *barbaricum* might entail determined efforts to overcome a series of strongpoints (the hillforts of the Dalmatians or the Durotriges of Britain, for example), some of which might not have succumbed immediately to a simple assault. In other campaigns (such as the conquest of Gaul), although sieges played a much more significant role, the main aim of the Roman army was to destroy the enemy's capacity to wage war. The investment of any given place might be undertaken in order to eliminate a hostile concentration (Mt. Medullus, 26 BC),[16] as a political demonstration/morale-sapping gesture (Avaricum, 52 BC),[17] or in order to remove a potential threat to extended communications and supply lines (Vellaunodunum, 52 BC).[18] It was also possible that a commander might mount a siege in response to an enemy's actions rather than through any deliberate initiative of his own. Thus Tiberius was compelled to besiege Dalmatian Andetrium (AD 9) to prevent Bato from using it as a secure base for guerrilla activity,[19] whilst Vercingetorix's occupation of Alesia (52 BC) served its purpose of luring Caesar into a difficult siege that might have resulted in a Roman disaster.

The notion of the siege as a trap for the unwary enemy, was also a well-practised Roman ruse. In this case, an investment was staged with the deliberate intention of provoking a general engagement with the enemy's field forces, whose efforts to relieve the beleaguered garrison might provide an opportunity for winning a decisive victory. This tactic was used with much success in Sulla's elimination of the Marian opposition in Italy, when several hostile concentrations were destroyed as they attempted to break the siege of Praeneste (82 BC).[20] Caesar too, was a keen exponent of this device, with the investment of Thapsus (46 BC) being designed to draw the allied army of Scipio and Juba into a decisive battle on favourable ground,[21] and his complex manoeuvring around Ategua (45 BC)[22] being intended to entice the cautious Gn. Pompeius into a full-scale engagement.

The allure of the 'final' battle might sometimes have persuaded commanders to commit themselves to sieges which stood little prospect of success, the Caesarian experience at

Dyrrachium (48 BC) providing a useful example. Here, despite Pompey's command of the sea and numerically superior forces, Caesar attempted to invest his enemy by the seizure and fortification of a number of key hill-top positions (*colour plate 1*) provoking a confused series of skirmishes and mêlées as each side contended for the high ground.[23] Although the general strategic position must have been perfectly clear to Caesar, he persisted with his efforts until his troops were over-stretched by the length of the line that they had to hold. In justifying his blockade, Caesar's reasoning remains only superficially plausible and his words fail to disguise the inherently risky nature of the scheme:

> First, that as he [Caesar] had a scanty supply of provisions and Pompey had a large preponderance of cavalry, he might be able to bring in for his army corn and stores from any direction at less risk; and also that he might prevent Pompey from foraging and might make his cavalry useless for active operations; and, thirdly, that he might diminish the moral influence on which Pompey seemed chiefly to rely among foreign nations, when the report should have spread throughout the world that he was being beleaguered by Caesar and did not dare to fight a pitched battle.[24]

That Caesar attempted such hazardous tactics at Dyrrachium, can probably be attributed to the confidence that he demonstrated in his troops, many of whom had participated in his Gallic campaigns and were familiar with the rapid extension of field works in the face of the enemy. However, Pompey too enjoyed the services of many veterans and with greater resources at his disposal, was more than capable of keeping abreast of the Caesarian design.

THE IMPORTANCE OF EXPERIENCE

It is self evident that troops who had long practice in siege work construction would be best equipped to undertake such works, particularly if time was an important consideration. Thus, when selecting troops for his forthcoming African campaign (205 BC), Publius Scipio chose men who had served with Marcellus at Syracuse as these would have been the best trained and most skilled in besieging cities.[25] Similarly, it is predictable that a unit of the calibre of the Tenth legion (which had participated in the campaign of suppression from its outset) was allocated the task of reducing the final centres of Jewish resistance after the fall of Jerusalem. The experience gained by its men in the art of ramp construction (at least two such structures being raised by its personnel during the siege of Jerusalem) was put to good use during the investment of Machaerus (AD 72) and Masada (AD 73). After both fortresses had been ringed by works of circumvallation, assault preparations were put in hand with the rapid extension of ramps against the enemy walls.

Apart from the degree of competence of the personnel detailed to undertake the construction of siege works, another important consideration would have been the ability of the commander to make appropriate tactical decisions. If a gifted general such as Caesar might make the occasional mistake (as at Gergovia or Dyrrachium), other, less experienced men could easily come to grief. When Cestius Gallus appeared before the walls of Jerusalem, he had several opportunities to conclude matters but his indecision prevented him from exploiting these properly.[26] Equally, Maximinus' short-term tactics of devastating the countryside around Aquileia (AD 238),[27] together with his inability to secure his supply lines and his failure to provide his troops with water that was fit to drink, all combined to result in disaster. However, perhaps the most striking example of poor generalship was evidenced by P. Claudius Pulcher during the second year (249 BC) of the siege of Lilybaeum. Although his predecessor had tried to seal the harbour against enemy blockade-runners, the depth of the water and the scouring action of the tides had prevented the success of the initiative. Even though he had not stepped shy of heaping scorn upon the tactic at the time, upon assuming command, Pulcher decided to renew the attempt. Once again, 'the sea hurled all to bits',[28] and the consul's wasted efforts drew censure in Diodorus' account as he 'repeated the mistakes of those whose leadership he had denounced, for he likewise reconstructed the jetties and barriers in the sea; his witlessness, however, outdid theirs insofar as the error of not being able to learn from experience is greater than that of being the first to try and fail'.[29]

Another aspect of experience that deserves attention is the question as to what degree prior knowledge of a given enemy, or of the physical environment in which the target was set, would have influenced the preparations for a siege action. We have already noted that Scipio's careful planning had taken account of the likely timber shortage in the vicinity of Numantia, but campaigns that were waged in still more hostile terrain would have demanded even greater foresight. In this respect, information gathered in the course of past campaigns may have provided useful intelligence so that when Julian launched his attack on Ctesiphon in AD 363 he took the precaution of outfitting a fleet to transport the necessary foodstuffs and matériel to accompany his army down the Euphrates. This sensible provision was made in the knowledge, presumably derived from earlier conflicts with the Sassanians, of the obstacles that lay in the path of advance and which would have been difficult to attack without such support.

Less care seemingly accompanied Severus' first attempt (AD 198) against Hatra (assuming that Dio's account of two separate attacks on the city is indeed correct), when his engines were burned and many troops were killed. The terse statement that Severus 'had accomplished nothing'[30] in this initial attack, may conceal intrinsic weaknesses in the planning of the operation and a failure to recall Trajan's experiences before the same city, when the lack of water, fodder and timber were all cited as excuses that made 'impossible a siege by a large multitude'.[31] However, this reverse did not discourage Severus from mounting a second attempt (AD 199?),[32] after a large stock of provisions had been gathered (perhaps a veiled suggestion that the first expedition had been under-supplied?) and many new engines constructed. Clearly Severus was of the opinion that a properly prepared army could reduce the city, notwithstanding the difficulties of the local environment, and events would demonstrate the accuracy of this confident assessment. Severus' knowledge of local conditions motivated him to advance his troops and machines against the city's powerful defences at the earliest opportunity as he was aware that the unhealthy climate was likely to spread disease through his large force. Despite heavy opposition, his men succeeded in breaching the enemy circuit on the nineteenth day of the operation, but a poor tactical decision to delay the assault allowed the Hatreni to raise new defences. When his troops refused to renew the attack on the following day Severus was compelled to raise the siege with victory in his grasp.

TOPOGRAPHICAL AND ENVIRONMENTAL CONSIDERATIONS

The Hatrene example illustrates how difficult environmental conditions did not necessarily preclude the prosecution of a siege, but issues of terrain, climate and the availability of natural resources would have exerted a powerful influence on the manner in which operations were pursued.

Although Caesar may have been reckless in undertaking the siege of Pompey's army at Dyrrachium, on other occasions he was very conscious of local topographical realities. At Avaricum, the river and marshes that ringed the site on all but a single, narrow front, made the task of a full-scale encirclement too impractical to contemplate,[33] whilst Gergovia, 'which was set upon a very lofty height, with difficult approaches on every side',[34] was too formidable a prospect for any storming party and would have been too dangerous to fully blockade when the Roman supply lines were under threat. Similarly, Vespasian's options at Gamala (AD 67) were also restricted by the precipitous slopes that bounded the town on three sides, and his resulting occupation 'of the mountain that overhung it'[35] was a strategy born out of necessity (4). When Aulus Albinus decided upon a surprise winter attack on the Jugurthine treasury at Suthul (109 BC),[36] his enthusiasm for securing a dramatic (and profitable) victory would seem to have clouded his judgment. When he arrived before the target, the strength of the position prevented any immediate escalade and the inclemency of the weather meant that any prolonged operation was out of the question. As his expedition now only carried the remotest possibility of success, Albinus should have retreated to winter quarters. Instead he decided to persist with his attack by starting the construction of an assault ramp, but his troops were drawn off and destroyed by Jugurtha's field army before this could be completed.

In several other cases, physical factors had a crucial effect on the outcome of campaigns. The ambitious attack launched by Metellus Pius against the town of Langobriga (79 BC),[37] despite its location deep in enemy territory, was predicated upon the Roman commander's expectation of a quick triumph. This confidence was based upon the intelligence received that there was only one well located within the town, the other water sources being extra-mural and easy to interrupt. However, the calculation that capitulation could be forced within two days proved hopelessly optimistic, as Sertorius not only contrived to send 2,000 water-skins to the defenders via little-used mountain paths, but also evacuated the 'useless mouths' from the town. At Delminium (156 BC), Roman forces under Figulus were frustrated by the steep slopes around the city which forestalled any attempt at an assault and made advancing engines an 'unprofitable' option,[38] persuading the commander to move elsewhere in search of an

4 Gamala from the east

easier target. Eventually when Figulus returned, he deployed his artillery around the site and fired incendiaries over the walls so that most of the town was destroyed in the ensuing conflagration. Although this approach may have been a product of Roman pique rather than any reasoned response to a difficult tactical situation, it cannot be disputed that the terrain was instrumental in influencing the course of events. Yet again, when the governor of Sicily was besieging rebel slaves on a hill near Halicyae (104 BC),[39] he realized that the strength of the position made the defenders immune to his relatively weak forces. Accordingly, instead of attempting more conventional approaches, he adopted a pragmatic stance and resorted to treachery to bring the affair to a conclusion. Finally, to illustrate the flexibility that climatic conditions might require, Julian's winter blockade of Frankish raiders in two abandoned forts on the banks of the Meuse (AD 357-358), was made secure by the deployment of patrol craft on the river in order to break up the ice flows that otherwise could have provided the enemy with an escape route.[40]

Other environmental factors might also influence the implementation of the chosen siege strategy. At Panormus (254 BC), for example, 'since the countryside (was) heavily wooded right up to the city gates', the consular armies proceeded to invest the city completely so that the palisade and trench were 'made to extend from sea to sea'.[41] The implication here suggests that such a work of circumvallation would not have been contemplated unless there had been plentiful natural resources available for exploitation in the vicinity. Similarly, Fulvius' decision to proceed with the siege of Ambracia (189 BC) depended (at least in part) upon the sufficiency of raw materials in the neighbourhood for the construction of his ramps and other works.[42] Of course, any reliance upon locally-obtained materials would have a direct impact on the nature and form of the resulting siege works. Accordingly, at sites such as Masada, where the nature of the terrain meant a scarcity of local timber resources, the assailants were obliged to maximize the use of stone in the building of the siege system. At times, this dependence on local resources might lead to unfortunate decisions. Thus, at Bezabde (AD 360), Constantius must have relied upon scavenging to provide the materials for his siege mounds as these were built of 'the branches of various trees, rushes and bundles of cane',[43] rather ramshackle-sounding structures which proved susceptible to Sassanian incendiary attack.

On an even more basic level, environmental constraints might sometimes be sufficiently pronounced as to determine whether (or at least, when) a siege might take place. For example, although Flavius Silva established long-range supply lines to bring up both water and provisions for the forces encircling Masada, it has been argued[44] that the siege could not have been commenced until late winter to early spring, when the rains would have filled the area's springs.

One specialized type of operation should be mentioned briefly at this stage, namely attacks against targets adjoining deep water that involved a significant naval element. Although much Roman effort could be directed at sealing enemy harbours by artificial means,[45] it was equally possible that a blockade might be enforced by a fleet maintaining its station offshore (for example, the arrival of Triarius' squadron successfully tightened the noose at Heraclea Pontica in 71 BC, even if the Mithridatic garrison was still able to flee the city by sea!).[46] The ships of the naval contingent might also provide more direct assistance to the attackers, particularly through the discharge of artillery against the walls (as when two galleys were lashed together at Utica, 204 BC, to provide a platform for the raising of a large tower),[47] or for the mounting of an escalade by marines against the walls (as during the siege of Syracuse, 214 BC).[48] But apart from such active measures, perhaps the greatest advantage conferred by a fleet was the flexibility that it offered by allowing the rapid deployment of men and equipment into the theatre of operations.

This was an advantage that was readily appreciated by Publius Scipio, when he planned the simultaneous juncture of his army and fleet before Carthago Nova (210 BC) in a dramatic demonstration of the Roman capacity to strike at will, deep within enemy territory. Control of the sea-lanes was also exploited during the offensive against Hannibal's bases in southern Italy. Thus when Crispinus sought to besiege Locri (208 BC), a fleet was amassed to attack the sea-facing walls and engines and artillery were brought over from Sicily.[49] Although Hannibal's approach forced the attempt to be curtailed, Cincius was later re-crossed from Sicily to resume the operation, his troops, in turn, being evacuated upon the Carthaginian's return for a second time. Even with the conclusion of Rome's wars of conquest around the Mediterranean littoral, occasional use was still made of the naval component in siege actions (e.g. to break the boom at Cyzicus, AD 365),[50] although these episodes usually had a riverine, rather than a maritime, character. These ranged from Octavian's use of river-craft at Siscia, 35 BC, to outflank the defences[51] to Julian's abortive attempt to emulate the vessel-borne tower from Utica at Aquileia, AD 361.[52]

Although many of the issues mentioned above deserve detailed treatment in their own right, further analysis of these matters remains beyond the scope of this book. However, the brief introduction provided here to the general context of Roman siege operations, does serve to indicate the range of contingent factors that might influence the chosen tactical approach. Of course, sieges did not take place in isolation (with even a campaign as specifically directed as that against Numantia involving preparatory manoeuvring to neutralize external threats), and the consideration of the individual siege work elements that follows should not obscure the importance of strategic and political factors to the understanding of why a particular target was subjected to attack. Furthermore, it should be remembered that the soldiers participating in reductive operations were not part of a specialist corps (even if some formations may, through practice, have acquired greater expertise than others), and, consequently, the question of the effectiveness or otherwise of their performance should be addressed in the broader context of general military training. In effect, the prosecution of siege operations was just one of the diverse range of skills that Roman military personnel were expected to acquire and, accordingly, the subject should not be divorced from the wider arena of Roman army studies.

POSTSCRIPT

www.psbooks.co.uk

6 BATTLE ROAD
HEATHFIELD ESTATE
NEWTON ABBOT TQ12 6RY UK
Postscript order line: +44 (0)1626 897100
Customer Services: +44 (0)1626 897123
Fax: +44 (0)1626 897129
email: enquiries@psbooks.co.uk
website: **www.psbooks.co.uk**

DESPATCH/ADVICE NOTE
Page 1

UK Hermes

Mr Colin Wharton

Date 03/12/2013
Despatch no. 4050433
Order no. 551298

62,oundle Drive,moulton
Northampton
Northants.
NN3 7DB

Ordered by customer 563459 - Mr Colin Wharton
Your ref: 131203163414-41354

WAREHOUSE LOCATION	CODE	QTY	DESCRIPTION		UNIT PRICE	TOTAL
B14B	92570	1	Roman Siege Works	9780752428970	6.99	6.99

Payment received with thanks:-
SAGE credit/debit card

8.99

*** Thank you for placing your order with Postscript. See our complete range of titles online at www.psbooks.co.uk ***

		£	
GOODS TOTAL			6.99
POST & PACKING			2.00
TOTAL		**£**	**8.99**

Weight:	Qty:	
0.41 kgs	1	
Picked by:	Packed by:	

Postscript is a division of Sandpiper Books Ltd
Registered in England No. 1715990

3

PREPARATORY WORKS

In the following chapters, the individual siege work elements of the Roman siege system are discussed in turn in order to obtain a clearer understanding of their function and the manner of their construction.

The mounting of a successful siege was largely the product of advance planning and of careful preparation, particularly if the target was located deep in hostile territory or in difficult terrain, or if the resistance of the defenders was prolonged. The dangers of under-preparation are clearly demonstrated by Maximinus' impetuous actions before Aquileia, where the short-sighted despoliation of the countryside and reliance on the contaminated river Natesio for the abstraction of water supplies meant that the besieging army was soon afflicted by famine and disease.[1] However, the comparative scarcity of references in our sources to such ill-prepared actions does suggest that Roman commanders appreciated that sieges demanded a major commitment of time and resources.

LOGISTICAL AND RELATED ISSUES

How to guarantee supply lines and obtain a sufficient stock of material with which to construct the intended siege works (and engines) were issues that the prudent commander would be wise to resolve before commencing his operations. Thus when M. Fulvius took the decision to lay siege to Ambracia (189 BC), he first satisfied himself that the city was susceptible to reduction on two counts: 'that there was both abundance of material close at hand for building mounds and raising other siege works, and a navigable river, the Aretho, suitable for the transportation of the necessary supplies, flowed past the very walls.'[2] That defenders understood the importance of locally available raw materials for construction purposes, can also be seen in the Xanthian decision (42 BC) to demolish their own suburbs to deny their use to Brutus, and in the preventative felling (and subsequent stockpiling within the walls) of the timber within a 6-mile radius by the Pompeian defenders of Ursao in Spain (45 BC), to discourage any Caesarian siege attempt.[3]

But the denial of raw materials from the immediate vicinity would not necessarily deter an assailant with sufficient foresight to have made suitable arrangements before the outset of the campaign. By way of illustration, an important aspect of Julian's Persian expedition (AD 363) was the outfitting of a fleet on the Euphrates, not only to transport food for the army but also the 'wood needed for siege equipment and some siege engines already constructed'.[4] This advance preparation allowed siege operations to be launched against centres of opposition encountered on the march to Ctesiphon that could otherwise have occasioned serious delay because of local scarcities of the necessary materials. Perhaps the most impressive testament to the efficacy of pre-planning can be seen in Metellus' attack (108 BC?) upon the desert city of Thala in Africa. This place had impressive defences, but its most obvious advantage lay in its isolation from the nearest extra-mural water supply, 50 miles away. Metellus was confident enough to undertake a full-scale siege of this centre, even employing the time-consuming expedients of circumvallation and siege mound construction, because his commissariat had arranged a train of water-carrying mules sufficient to sustain his troops throughout the 40-day operation.[5]

Of course, it would always have been easier to guarantee sufficient supplies when a campaign was launched with the specific objective of eliminating a particular target. For example, the concentration of three separate Roman field armies to reduce Capua (212-211 BC), meant that the consuls took the precaution of fortifying nearby towns to act as granaries that could then be filled by the Sardinian grain fleet to ensure the provisioning of the besiegers over the winter.[6] But the impact of supply considerations might be harder to anticipate in the course of a general campaign, where sudden shortages might force a rapid revision of the strategic plan. This can be seen on three separate occasions during Caesar's suppression of Vercingetorix's revolt (52 BC). Firstly, the *oppidum* of Vellaunodunum was invested in order to remove a strategic threat to the army supply lines;[7] secondly, the siege of Avaricum was delayed by the necessity of making a demonstration against the camp of the Gallic field army (to deter enemy cavalry from interfering with foraging parties);[8] and thirdly, the explanation that Caesar gives[9] for not mounting a full blockade of Gergovia was the necessity of ensuring the security of his corn supply. In this last instance, the uncertain military situation in the hinterland deterred Caesar from throwing a line of investment around the target as he realized that, if he marched away to engage a hostile threat in his rear, any remaining garrison would be vulnerable to a sudden sortie. Indeed, when this threat did materialize, and Caesar was obliged to remove two-thirds of the army to deal with it, the troops left behind to hold the extended blockade camp were hard pressed to maintain their positions, justifying the original assessment.[10]

The paramount need to ensure a continuity of supplies to the besieging force was one of the most pressing reasons behind Vespasian's order to improve the road from Ptolemais to Iotapata (AD 67) at the outset of his Galilean campaign, notwithstanding Josephus' statement that the task of levelling (presumably, grading) this road was to make it practicable for the Roman cavalry.[11]

Trajan's experience before Hatra (AD 117?) can be cited as a case study of how an ill-conceived and poorly-planned operation could lead to disaster, as the sub-text to Dio's account of the 'repulse' suffered at the hands of the Hatreni implies. The excuse that Hatra was surrounded by desert and had no ready supply of water, timber or fodder 'making impossible a siege by a large multitude'[12] seems to be an attempt to conceal the lack of preparation that accompanied the venture. The geographical isolation of the city was well known to the Romans and to attempt a siege without the provision of an adequate logistical train suggests that the emperor did not expect to encounter serious resistance. This impression is reinforced by the report that Trajan first sent his cavalry out against the city, an unconventional siege tactic at best, indicating an apparent belief that a demonstration in force would suffice to overawe the defenders. Clearly, the mere presence of the emperor was insufficient to intimidate the Hatreni and the Romans found themselves committed to a siege for which they were inadequately prepared (cf. Severan operations against the same target in AD 198 and 199). Given the difficult nature of the terrain, it was always unlikely that such an action would succeed in the absence of a properly organized commissariat.

SITE RECONNAISSANCE AND INTELLIGENCE GATHERING

In order to decide whether siege operations were possible and, if so, what manner of siege system should be employed, the commander of the attacking forces had to assess the nature of the terrain in the vicinity of the target. No doubt the best appreciation of topographical reality could be obtained by direct, personal observation in line with Onasander's recommendation[13] that a general should always 'skilfully inspect the camp of the enemy', although our sources rarely confirm that such surveys took place. However, it appears that Flamininus and his tribunes carried out a detailed reconnaissance at Sparta (195 BC)[14] by riding around the (incomplete) walls as did M. Acilius Glabrio at Heraclea (191 BC),[15] whilst Julian undertook a careful inspection of the defences of Maiozamalcha (AD 363).[16] In other cases it is obvious that the commander had made a similar assessment. Having been persuaded by his Epirote allies that Ambracia was vulnerable to siege (for the reasons mentioned above), when Fulvius appeared before the target he quickly appreciated that its formidable site and fortifications would involve his troops in much labour.[17] Similarly, Caesar's inspection of the terrain at Avaricum (52 BC) led him to conclude that it ruled out the possibility of a work of circumvallation and persuaded him to adopt a blockade camp as the more effective approach.[18]

In some instances it is apparent that commanders took insufficient care over their initial site survey, resulting in unfortunate tactical decisions. The site selected by Censorinus for his camp on the stagnant lagoon before Carthage (149 BC)[19] is an example. After being in position for some time, and having been weakened both by heavy labour and hard fighting, his troops started to fall sick in their unhealthy bivouacs, compelling the relocation of the Roman camp to the open seashore. If Harmand is correct in his analysis,[20] even an astute commander such as Caesar was not above poor tactical assessments, as the first, abandoned stretches of contravallation at Alesia would seem to demonstrate (colour plate 5). However, the ambiguous nature of the archaeological evidence may exonerate Caesar from any charge of negligence, as it is equally possible that these discontinuous ditches may have fulfilled the initial purpose of sheltering the Roman work parties from interference by the Gallic cavalry.[21] Once Vercingetorix had ordered the evacuation of his horsemen, these covering works would have lost their utility in any event.

Josephus records an unusual episode when he states that Titus only made a detailed reconnaissance of the best place to attack Jerusalem (AD 70) *after* a number of preparatory measures had been put in hand.[22] As these involved the careful concentration of the converging army columns in three separate camps, the levelling of the approaches to the walls and the subsequent relocation of two of the legionary bases in closer proximity to the enemy, it is fair to assume that Titus had already made a judicious evaluation of the terrain before carrying out his reported reconnaissance to determine the tactical *point d' appui*.

ENCAMPMENT

One of the most pressing concerns for any besieging commander would have been to ensure the safety of his army immediately upon its arrival before a target by selecting and fortifying a suitable site in the vicinity. It should be noted that the discussion here is limited to those aspects of castrametation directly relevant to the initial stages of a siege campaign. More permanent works of encampment (i.e. works that were intended to be an active element of the siege system) are covered in the next chapter.

Temporary field fortifications that provided the army with cover upon arrival were particularly important when the defenders adopted an aggressive posture. Thus, at Sparta (195 BC),[23] Nabis led his troops out of the city and engaged Flamininus' men as they were busy pitching camp causing great confusion in the Roman ranks. Unfortunately for the Spartans, this success was not fully exploited and an attempt to repeat the manoeuvre on the following day (after the Roman camp had been completed) resulted in the repulse of the sortie with heavy losses. In a similar manner, when the Tenth legion arrived before Jerusalem (AD 70), it took up an isolated position on the Mount of Olives 6 stades from the city but screened by the steep-sided Kidron Valley.[24] However, this natural obstacle was insufficient to deter the defenders from sallying out whilst the legionaries were dispersed in various work parties engaged in camp construction. Without the rapid despatch of reinforcements from Titus' main position on Mount Scopus, it is likely that this furious attack would have resulted in the piecemeal destruction of the legion. Although the Tenth legion thereafter remained *in situ* on the Mount of Olives (with its camp presumably strengthened to become a permanent work), the timing of the Jewish attack to coincide with the initial occupation of the position, demonstrates the vulnerability of construction details working in exposed positions during the opening phases of a siege.

That the Romans improvised temporary field works upon their arrival at the intended target is predictable given that it was considered good practice[25] for camps to be built whenever the army halted for the night, particularly if an enemy was known to be in the vicinity. Accordingly, it is not difficult to find references that confirm the adoption of this sensible policy by commanders. Upon Scipio Aemilianus' appearance before Numantia, the construction of two camps was immediately put in hand, a procedure for which his troops had been intensively drilled before the outset of the campaign[26] and facilitated by the seven stakes[27] carried to the site by each soldier (allowing the encampments to

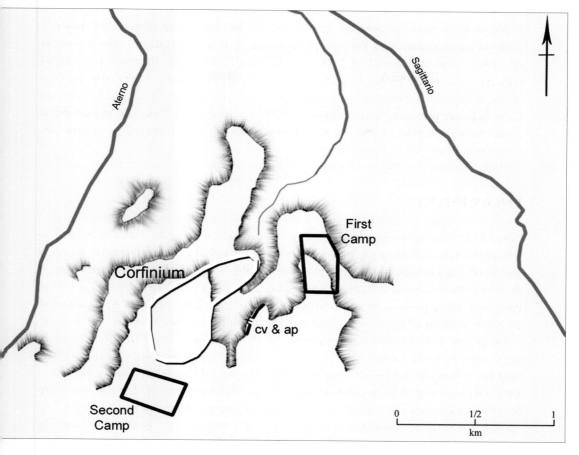

Aterno

Sagittario

First
Camp

Corfinium

cv & ap

Second
Camp

0   1/2   1

km

5 The siege system at Corfinium indicating possible section of circumvallation (cv) and artillery position (ap)

be rapidly completed without awaiting the scavenging of material from the surrounding countryside). The existence of previous Roman camps on the hill of Castillejo,[28] Scipio's putative headquarters, may have influenced the choice of that particular site, although it is unlikely that any earlier structures would have survived Numantine demolition. Again, when Caesar moved against Corfinium (49 BC) he pitched camp 'next to the wall' to await the arrival of the rest of his forces.[29] Without sufficient troops to confront the large Pompeian garrison, Caesar's first action was to guarantee the security of his position by prompt fortification (5).

Although in both these examples, the first sites chosen for encampment were subsequently retained as part of the general siege system, in some instances initial positions were soon abandoned in favour of locations more relevant to the operational plan. For example, Titus relocated his first two camps on Mount Scopus to positions much closer to the enemy in front of the Hippicus and Psephinus towers[30] respectively (although observation posts, at least, must have remained at the original sites), whilst

Julian's first camp at Maiozamalcha (AD 363) was supplanted by another, better-placed encampment[31] on the second day of the siege.

SCREENING WORKS

The vulnerability of working parties to sudden hostile sorties was not restricted to the initial camp construction phase, as an active enemy might continue to disrupt siege preparations by attacking any exposed construction details. A good example of the potential of a well-timed sally can be seen during Servilianus' siege of Erisana (c.141 BC), when a dawn assault launched from the town succeeded in surprising and routing the Roman troops who were busily engaged in trench digging.[32] Clearly, Servilianus had not taken the appropriate precautions to prevent (or at least deter) such an eventuality, but other, more prudent commanders were careful to provide cover for their labour parties.

Perhaps the simplest means of affording protection was to advance a cordon of troops to shield the pioneers from any direct attack. This tactic was employed by Titus at Jerusalem, when selected men were posted ahead of the teams engaged in the ground levelling operation that preceded the transfer of the camps from Scopus.[33] Given the scale of the clearance works, this screening body needed to have been sufficiently numerous to intimidate the besieged, as the internal dissension that wracked the competing factions within the walls (diverting attention from the Roman manoeuvres) could not have been guaranteed to last. The importance of this screening role was underlined by the selection of Titus' best troops to provide the necessary cover.

However, in circumstances where the enemy were less distracted and were sufficiently numerous, the protective value of any forward-stationed troop cordon might be strengthened either by the careful use of terrain or by the addition of artificial defences. In the first of these circumstances, advantage might be taken of favourable local topography as occurred at Ambracia, where Fulvius' work parties were sheltered by the fortuitous course of the River Aretho.[34] Another possibility would be to seize and garrison an extra-mural suburb that might then serve to contain any enemy sortie. As we have seen, the desire to prevent Brutus from obtaining some such lodgement was one of the reasons that motivated the Xanthians to destroy their own suburbs. Such conveniences of nature, or of urban planning, were unlikely to be encountered very often, and besiegers would usually have to rely upon artificial methods of providing cover for their construction teams.

One of the better-known examples of deliberate screening works was the scheme employed by Scipio Aemilianus at Numantia. Here, having planted his forts on the commanding heights, Scipio ordered the construction of a ditch and palisade around the town and instituted a field signalling system to give warning of any hostile sortie.[35] It was only after this initial investment had been completed and he could 'effectively repel any assaults' that Scipio pressed ahead with the building of a line of circumvallation to link the encircling forts. In the course of his investigations, Schulten could not find any trace of this screening work[36] and he speculated, quite reasonably, that a ditch would only have been necessary on the eastern plain (colour plate 4), with the Tera, Merdancho and Duero rivers acting in a similar capacity on the other flanks. Although Schulten also suggests that the shallow waters of the Tera may have required reinforcement by a stockade line, the water flow in the autumnal conditions would have made a sudden crossing difficult.

Archaeological evidence does exist, however, for the forward work referred to by Caesar[37] as a shield for his construction details during the siege of Alesia. Here, 'he dug a ditch 20ft wide with perpendicular sides, in such fashion that the bottom thereof was just as broad as the distance from edge to edge at the surface'. Although this feature was 'confirmed' by the Napoleonic excavations, when it was revisited in more recent times,[38] the dimensions and profile of the ditch given by Caesar were seen to be exaggerated, with the modern section producing a profile 3.1m wide and c.1m deep beneath the plough soil (although the latter dimension may reflect truncation by later activity). It has been argued[39] that this advance trench across the plaine des Laumes (colour plate 5) formed part of a general screening system, the other elements of which comprised the Oze and Ozerain streams which flow to the north and south of the oppidum respectively, with the east being sealed by a length of ditch cutting across the col linking Mt Pennevelle with Mt Auxois. Although this is an interesting hypothesis, there is insufficient evidence to support its conclusions: the ditch that cuts across the col does not share the same profile (or width) as the feature that crosses the plaine des Laumes[40] whilst neither of the two streams would have much delayed troops intent upon their fording. As previously observed however, the various short stretches of discontinuous ditch that are located beneath the surrounding hills as well as in the plaine de Grésigny may have some claim to be treated as screening works, albeit that their intermittent nature suggests that they served as ad hoc local responses rather than forming part of an integrated screening system for the entire circuit of investment.

In respect of the 'ditch of 20ft', Caesar further states that he set the other siege works back from it at a range of 400ft (although 'paces' might be more accurate) as the actual interval between this obstacle and the line of contravallation in the plaine des Laumes varies from 200m to 950m.[41] Conveniently, Caesar tells us why he considered it necessary to build this preliminary barrier:

> for as he had of necessity included so large an area, and the whole of the works could not easily be manned by a ring-fence of troops, his intention was to provide against any sudden rush of the enemy's host by night upon the entrenchments, or any chance of directing their missiles by day upon our troops engaged on the works.[42]

Presumably the hard-fought cavalry engagement that had ranged over the same ground as that now obstructed by the 'ditch of 20ft', had influenced Caesar's assessment, although Vercingetorix's premature decision to evacuate his horsemen had reduced the threat of a sudden descent on the Roman works.

Perhaps the most extreme manifestation of this concern to provide some form of temporary protection to the besieging army can be seen at Munda (45 BC), where a palisade was extemporized from shields and javelins planted on top of a 'rampart' of corpses dragged from the nearby battlefield.[43] This grisly tableau was soon replaced by a more formal system of conventional entrenchments once the siege was pursued in a more organized fashion.

CLEARANCE AND DEMOLITION

As part of initial security and supply considerations, it was sometimes necessary for the besieging commander to undertake preparatory ground clearance measures to ensure the smooth progress of his operation. Although such works might also have been required as a preliminary to siege work construction (particularly the raising of a ramp/mound), we will restrict the discussion here to clearance/demolition processes undertaken at the outset of the campaign.

One of the more common reasons for undertaking clearance and ground preparation, was to provide the army with a level and accessible field of operations. This would allow the unrestricted deployment of a variety of engines, an open avenue of advance (and, if necessary, of retreat) and an unobstructed view of the course of events. A further benefit might be the intimidation of the defenders through the destruction of their familiar landscapes.[44]

When Titus took the decision to move his camps from Mount Scopus closer to the walls of Jerusalem, he ordered his army to level the intervening ground behind the cover of a screening force. Consequently, in four days, all the suburban gardens were swept away, all the trees were felled, gullies were filled in and any protruding rocks were prised out with iron tools. With the advantage of an open field of battle, which allowed the simultaneous deployment of seven ranks of troops to guard against any sortie, the army baggage and the siege train were then moved to take up position in the new camps opposite the Hippicus and Psephinus towers. If the record in Josephus[45] is accurate, this relocation of the army from Scopus to the opposite side of the city (6) must have been a very laborious undertaking, as the levelling of the 'intervening ground' must have involved the razing of the extra-mural suburbs both north and east of the district of Bezetha. That the dangerous manoeuvre of exposing the flank of the army to enemy attack was completed without incident, should probably be attributed to the internal dissension that paralysed the defenders' responses as the opportunity to strike at this vulnerable time would surely not have been deterred by the simple presence of screening forces however strongly drawn up. Presumably Titus' decision to undertake this manoeuvre was influenced by intelligence reports that indicated the degree to which internal conflict had temporarily incapacitated any co-ordinated efforts by the defenders.

The advantage of ground preparation to ease the advance of an army would have been made clear to Titus from the manner in which his father had proceeded at Gamala (AD 67). With precipitous slopes making a complete investment impossible (7), Vespasian was forced to prepare for an attack across the saddle that connected the town to the massif immediately to its east. Two of his legions were engaged in camp construction and in isolating the town by means of entrenchments while the third filled in the trenches and ravines that fronted the one practicable approach. Josephus' account[46] indicates that these various measures were rapidly completed, allowing engines to be moved forward against the enemy wall, although the Jewish defenders on the ramparts managed to delay this deployment until they were driven off by a sustained artillery bombardment. The positive approach adopted towards the reduction of Gamala can be contrasted with the ineffectual siege that the Roman client Agrippa II, had mounted for the preceding seven

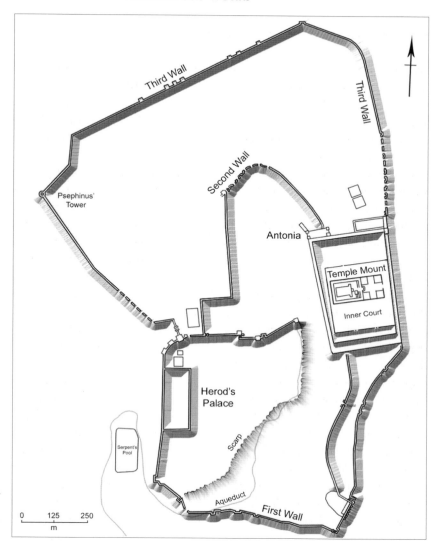

6 Jerusalem in AD 70. *After Bahat 1990*

months.[47] In view of the preparatory works instituted by Vespasian, this was likely a passive affair in which no thought was given to forcing the issue by means of an assault (although the troops at Agrippa's disposal were always likely to have been limited).

Another advantage deriving from a systematic programme of clearance, was the resulting harvest of raw materials that might be usefully employed in subsequent siege work construction. This was particularly true when extra-mural suburbs were demolished. At Jerusalem for example, as much timber as possible was salvaged from the razed settlements beyond the 'Third' wall for use in Titus' first set of offensive earthworks. But timber was only one of many different elements that the demolition process might yield. At Heraclea (191 BC) we are told[48] that 'not only beams and planks but brick and cement and stones of different sizes' were all recovered from the ravaging of the suburbs

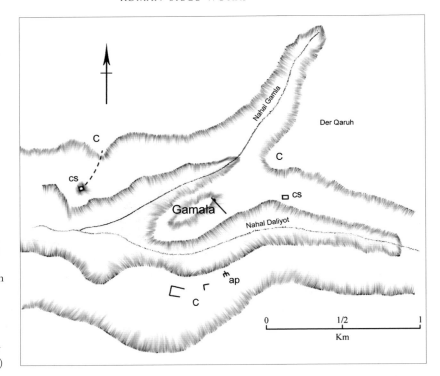

7 The siege system at Gamala with possible Roman camps (C), castella (cs) and artillery position (ap)

by Acilius' men, materials that were subsequently recycled in the various works advanced against the city. There was, of course, nothing new in such a tactic, with the debris of a demolished extra-mural temple being employed to raise the Persian assault ramp at Palaepaphos,[49] and a consciousness of the utility of such materials was a further reason given for the Xanthian decision to raze their own suburbs.

These various preparatory works were very much the product of advanced planning by the besieging commander and would have served as a useful (in some cases, vital) preliminary to the commencement of the formal siege operation. From the end of the first century AD, the increasing tendency for sieges to be mounted on a more *ad hoc* basis and the greater preoccupation with the methods of assault, meant that the careful provision of a siege-conducive environment became progressively rarer. Whilst such measures as Aurelian's tampering with the loyalty of the *saracenoi* who might otherwise have ambushed the supply caravans for his troops before Palmyra (AD 272)[50] or Julian's provision of a flotilla to support his campaign down the Euphrates (AD 363),[51] may stand out as exceptional examples of forward planning, there is no further record of specific engineering works being undertaken as a preliminary to the construction of a siege system. Although this may reflect prevailing textual weaknesses, it is more likely to be a true reflection of the adoption of less methodical siege strategies.

Having outlined the measures that might be instituted in the first hours or days of a siege operation, we will now turn to the works undertaken subsequently which were more directly relevant to the implementation of the chosen siege system.

4

BLOCKADE CAMPS

The first component of the siege system that we will discuss will be the 'blockade camp'. For sake of clarity, a blockade camp(s) may be defined as a fortified position (or set of positions) established by the besieger, with or without connecting branches or spurs (*bracchia*). The function of the blockade camp is threefold: to prevent the re-supply or reinforcement of a defended centre; to deter any sortie or foraging effort mounted from the same; and to serve as a garrison base for the besieging force. This type of siege work is distinguishable from a circumvallation by the fact that it does not attempt to provide a hermetic seal via a continuous line of investment but seeks to maintain a blockade by looser means, making it more economical both in terms of labour input and garrison requirement. Given that this method of control was not based upon a linear cordon, its efficacy demanded that the besieging army had to intervene in the field to prevent the infiltration or exfiltration of hostile forces. The defences of the camp might also provide a secure place of retreat in the event of any reverse. To this extent, the blockade camp operated very much in the same way as the usual conception of the Roman 'playing card' fort, where the emphasis was on its role as a base for forward power projection rather than as a passive provider of point defence.

THE ROMAN USE OF BLOCKADE CAMPS

The provision of a fortified encampment to act as a secure base of operations for a besieging force must have been a commonplace of ancient siege warfare and Roman armies engaged in siege operations would scarcely have neglected such an elementary precaution. However, in order for an encampment to be treated here as a blockade work rather than as a simple field camp, it is necessary to demonstrate that it was designed to fulfil the objectives outlined above. Suggestive evidence might include some indication that the camp was designed to last for the duration of the siege campaign, that it had particularly elaborate defences, or that it was favourably sited for the enforcement of the blockade.

Although it is doubtful that we should place much faith in the accounts of the earliest Roman sieges (see chapter 1), it is notable that the operations before Fidenae (620s BC),[1] Corniculum (*c.*600 BC),[2] Ardea (*c.*510 BC)[3] and Corioli (493 BC),[4] would all seem to have featured blockade camps. The last example is particularly instructive as the besiegers are portrayed as splitting their forces to resist a simultaneous attack mounted by a Volscian relief column and the enemy garrison. That one detachment marched out of the camp to engage the external threat, whilst the remainder took up position to repulse the hostile sortie from the defences would seem to encapsulate the *raison d'être* of the blockade camp.

It is reasonable to suppose that blockade camps became a standard element of the siege repertoire, at least in long, drawn-out operations. Thus at Veii (405-396 BC), the construction of the first ever Roman *hibernacula*[5] served to demonstrate the determination of the assailants, even if that meant holding fast during the winter months rather than evacuating the field at the close of the campaigning season. Similar winter quarters were also established at Palaeopolis (327-326 BC), Saticula (316-315 BC) and Bovianum (313 BC).[6]

As campaigns became more protracted, it is likely that blockade camps would have become progressively more elaborate to reflect increasingly complex tactical situations. The system constructed to contain the Veientes, involving fixed *castra* and satellite *castella*,[7] is probably best interpreted as representing this more evolved form of blockade camp rather than a methodical attempt at circumvallation. Other hints[8] that supplementary works were added to the basic fortified bases at Palaeopolis and Saticula imply that blockade camps were now thought of as the anchor points of an integrated system.

Certainly, the set-piece sieges of Agrigentum (262 BC) and Lilybaeum (250-249 BC)[9] during the First Punic War would seem to suggest this new tactical approach, with the incidence of multiple blockade camps connected by *bracchia* illustrating the sophistication of the siege schema employed at both sites. Although these 'extended' blockade camp systems were subsequently converted into full circumvallatory works, this was not the original intention of the besiegers. At Agrigentum, the conversion process would appear to have been accretional, with a series of 'organic' developments eventually resulting in the isolation of the city, whilst at Lilybaeum, the failure of various assaults led to the decision to leave the 'result to time'[10] via the construction of a continuous line of investment.

The advantageous concentration of force against hostile threats that a blockade camp system made possible, would certainly seem to have been the motivation that persuaded Marcellus to abandon his attenuated blockade of Syracuse (214-212 BC) in favour of a consolidated army base situated some distance from the Hexapylon Gate.[11] This prevented any close supervision of the besieged (allowing individuals and small parties to infiltrate/exfiltrate without too much difficulty), but ensured that the siege could still be maintained on a strategic level and reduced the threat of a sudden attack overwhelming any isolated besieging detachment.

The transition towards the adoption of circumvallation as the preferred vehicle of isolation (see chapter 5) meant that the blockade camp became an increasingly specialized tool in the siege repertoire, chosen in circumstances where the topography so dictated, or where manpower resources were insufficient to furnish an adequate garrison for a complete encirclement. The camp that Publius Scipio constructed as a base before Carthago Nova (210 BC)[12] reflected a careful terrain assessment, as despite the simplicity of the task (with a narrow isthmus only 250 paces wide), it was decided not to cut off the city by artificial means, but to encamp on raised ground further back. This allowed Scipio to retain the flexibility of an open field of operations whilst his rear remained protected against enemy relief attempts launched from the hinterland. Furthermore, had the isthmus been directly blocked, then the bluffs behind would have required garrisoning nonetheless to prevent their seizure by hostile forces. The blockade camp option, therefore, remained the economical choice in manning terms.

Despite the rationale behind the location of the blockade camp at Carthago Nova, in other cases of topographical constraint it would seem that besieging commanders made maximum use of the terrain to ensure that their chosen base sealed any practicable (landward) approach to the target. At Carthage (147 BC) for example, the evacuation of the Carthaginian outworks allowed Scipio Aemilianus to occupy the whole of the isthmus connecting the city to the mainland and to block the same by means of his quadrangular 'long fort'.[13] Similarly, at Avaricum (52 BC),[14] Caesar commenced his operation by pitching camp across the narrow corridor of dry land which formed the only possible axis of advance, the other flanks being covered by natural obstacles.

The continuing utility of blockade camps where the terrain was favourable, can be demonstrated at Nahal Hever, in the course of the suppression of the Bar Kokhba revolt (c.AD 135). Here, two camps (8 and 9) were built on the cliff-edge on either side of the precipitous wadi of Nahal Hever, situated so as to overlook the cave mouths set in the opposite cliff-faces. As certain of these caves (the 'Cave of Letters' and the 'Cave of Horror') were occupied by guerrillas,[15] the forts allowed surveillance of the cave entrances and signals passed from one to the other would have warned of any attempted breakout. Given the impracticality of the sheer descent from the caves to the wadi bottom, the carefully positioned Roman camps both prevented any escape attempt and severed the only route to the one possible water source,[16] making the enemy positions untenable for any length of time.

Blockade camps might also be built where the assailant was faced with a shortage of troops. This would certainly appear to have been the reason behind Caesar's tactics in establishing camps at Gergovia (52 BC), where a complete investment would have resulted in the over-extension of his available forces, and at Corfinium (49 BC), where his arrival with the van of the army meant that he had insufficient troops to undertake the task of encirclement. At the latter site, when the rest of his army eventually came up, Caesar established a second camp on the other side of the town and the necessary work to surround the target with a line of circumvallation was then put in hand.

If Vegetius' fourth-century report is to be believed that field fortifications were no longer constructed whilst the army was on the march, as 'the knowledge of this technique has altogether perished',[17] then it is not surprising that blockade camps too, would seem to fade from the record during the later empire. In a recent monograph concerning the temporary camps of England,[18] there is a conspicuous (if understandable) failure to address this question of chronological range, even though the detailed treatment of a specific geographical area would have been the ideal forum in which to test the accuracy of Vegetius' statement. That the remark is not the rhetorical exaggeration that some would argue[19] may be indicated by the specific way in which Ammianus Marcellinus emphasizes

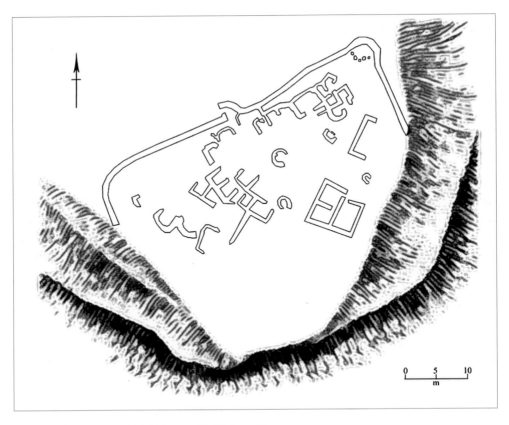

8 Blockade camp A at Nahal Hever. *After Yadin 1963b*

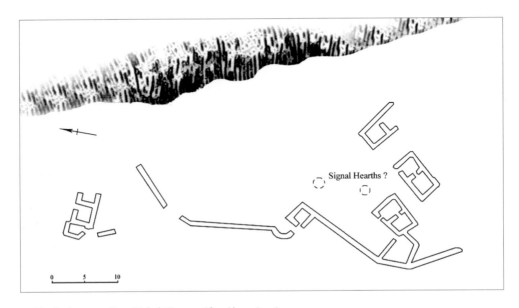

9 Blockade camp B at Nahal Hever. *After Aharoni 1961*

the process of camp construction undertaken at the sieges of Bezabde (AD 360),[20] Maiozamalcha (AD 363)[21] and the fort near Ctesiphon (AD 363).[22] Here, the impression is given of unusual measures being undertaken to combat the militarily proficient Persians.

It is the structural attributes of the blockade camp that we will now turn to.

FORM AND STRUCTURE

The discussion here will be restricted to those matters that are directly relevant to the construction of blockade camps, and for a more considered treatment of the general process of castrametation, the reader is advised to look elsewhere.[23] As a result, the writings of Hyginus and Vegetius, that relate to the various considerations applicable to questions of camp siting, construction and layout will not be specifically addressed, although much the same principles must also have informed the methodology of blockade camp provision.

It is apparent from both the literary sources and from the limited archaeological evidence that blockade camps could assume a wide variety of forms depending upon the scale of the operation and the precise roles that the works were intended to fulfil. It is probably fair to suppose that the earliest examples would have comprised simple palisaded and/or ditched enclosures having a similar character to the 'marching camps' of a later period, although the *stativus* claimed for the siege of Ardea, might have had enhanced defences if it represented a more 'permanent' type of encampment.

That early blockade camps were capable of resisting an enemy attack, is suggested by the repulse of the sortie launched by the defenders of Corioli. More critical however, was the situation at Veii, where determined resistance and the ever-present threat of intervention from Etruria meant that the siege was always a rather precarious affair. We have already seen in chapter 1 how the textual accounts of this episode are likely to have been coloured by anachronism and how the portrayal of a comprehensive line of circumvallation encircling the city seems improbable given the alleged duration of the investment. Accordingly, in these circumstances, it may be preferable to interpret the various works that were constructed in the vicinity as representing an elaborate extended blockade camp system, although the suggestions that follow as to its composition must be regarded as conjectural.

It seems that operations began conventionally enough with the army appearing before Veii during the campaigning season of 405 BC, although the diversion of forces to fight the Volsci in the following year resulted in the scaling back of the Roman effort. A renewed concentration against the city was seen in 403 BC, with the potential for external interference prompting the besiegers to construct their works 'as to have a double fortification, one facing Veii, to oppose the sallies of the townsfolk, the other confronting Etruria, to shut off any assistance that might come from thence'.[24] The character of this work must remain ambiguous, but it is possible that it comprised two parallel entrenchments that linked separate Roman camps. Some of Appius Claudius' speech,[25] therefore, may have been based on reality, with the existence of a *vallum fossaque*, forts and earthworks facing Etruria, all being explicable within this limited context. The seriousness of Roman intentions (and, presumably, the reluctance to abandon siege works built with such effort) was signalled by the construction of *hibernacula*[26] to sustain the troops over winter. This may have involved the conversion of one of the existing blockade camps or the construction of a completely new structure to act as a consolidated base for the whole besieging force.

The operation suffered a serious setback in 402 BC, when a simultaneous attack was launched against the Roman works by both the besieged and a relief army. Poor co-ordination led to the Roman army being defeated in detail, with the attackers succeeding in scaling the ramparts[27] and in storming various *castella*, compelling the besiegers to seek refuge in their 'larger camp'.[28] The crucial factor that resulted in the breaching of the blockade system was the failure of the Roman generals to lead their men out of the works to confront one or other of the attacking formations. Rather, it would seem a passive defence was attempted, which led to the rolling up of each position in turn as it was exposed to an attack in overwhelming force. From this, we can infer that the Roman system comprised two main 'camps' or *castra* (the larger of which acted as the rallying point) and a series of strongpoints (*castella*) perhaps linked by the double entrenchment previously mentioned. As the enemy managed to scale the defences with relative ease, it is unlikely that these connecting earthworks were crowned with any battlements (certainly, none are mentioned), and it is entirely possible that these were only designed to act as obstacles rather than as fighting platforms.

As refuge was taken in the 'larger' of the Roman camps, it is clear that there were two main garrison bases. Given that the *hibernacula* needed to have been of sufficient size to hold the whole of the army over the winter, it is reasonable to equate this with the *maiora castra* that acted as the *reduit* for the whole complex. This identification is strengthened by the fact that the Romans were able to maintain their control of this position, perhaps in consequence of the enhanced defences provided for the winter quarters. Although this defeat was a significant check to Roman ambitions, it also testified to the overall efficacy of the blockade camp concept as the Veientes and their allies were unable to overthrow the blockade despite this tactical success.

In 400 BC the Romans managed to recover their 'lost camp', a reference to the second, smaller garrison base seized at the time of the successful sortie and they subsequently sought to reinforce their positions with 'forts and camps'.[29] The most convincing explanation has the strategy reverting to a simple blockade maintained from the single camp left in Roman possession after the defeat of 402 BC until the successful counter-attack allowed the besiegers to restore their original design.

The besieged attempted to repeat their previous success in the following year, when another sally was mounted upon the appearance of a second relief army. On this occasion, whilst the besiegers maintained resistance from around their works,[30] a column was despatched from the main camp to fall upon the exposed rear of the Etruscan field army. This action demonstrates how the blockade camp system was meant to work, the Romans having absorbed the danger of passive point defence. Despite this victory, the siege continued to drag on inconclusively until Camillus mounted a preclusive offensive in Etruria to deter any further relief attempts. The siege works were then strengthened by the addition of further redoubts (no doubt improving the supervision and maintenance of the blockade) and the affair was brought to a conclusion via the stratagem of a secret gallery driven under the enemy walls.

If we believe the Livian narrative that such a complex system was employed at Veii (without parallel elsewhere for another century-and-a-half), this can probably be attributed to the proximity of the target to the city of Rome. After all, sustaining a protracted siege of this nature must have been much easier when the supply lines were short and the source of reinforcement was close to hand. One potential lesson that Veii may have demonstrated however, was the utility of the 'extended' blockade camp concept, where the base was regarded as the anchor point for a series of satellite works. These satellites may only have comprised the sentry posts for a picquet cordon and probably remained unconnected by any linking work, but the adoption of the principle of detached troop deployment in fixed positions was a significant step towards the prosecution of a more effective siege.

Other early experiments in this direction can be identified at both Palaeopolis (327-326 BC) and Saticula (316-315 BC). At the former site, the Roman commander interposed his army between the allied communities of Palaeopolis and Neapolis and, by encamping on the intervening ground, he prevented any co-ordination in the resistance. This separation was made even more emphatic by the construction of entrenchments which probably comprised either branch-works or *castella* to sever the communications between the two centres.[31] The presence of a Samnite garrison of 4,000 at Palaeopolis suggests that these Roman works would have been sufficiently well protected to contain any hostile sortie. At Saticula, after the battle that resulted when the army was led out to confront a combined attack from both the townsfolk and an external column, the new dictator took the precaution of outposting detachments to ensure that his camp was shielded from further unexpected attack.[32]

However, it was not until the First Punic War that the degree of sophistication seen in the works employed before Veii were again revisited, with the sieges of the important Carthaginian centres of Agrigentum (262 BC) and Lilybaeum (250-241 BC) providing the *raison d'être* for such elaboration.

At the former city, a substantial Roman/allied army of 100,000 men pitched one large camp at a distance of 8 stades from the enemy walls[33] and foragers were sent out to secure supplies for what was anticipated would be a long campaign. A Carthaginian attack upon these dispersed units succeeded in forcing them to retreat to the encampment from which the sally was firmly repulsed. This much might be expected of the standard blockade camp, but the confidence that this success engendered encouraged the subsequent Roman initiative to divide the army and to set up a second camp on the opposite side of the city allowing a closer supervision of the blockade. The decision to link both camps by means of entrenchments with fortified garrison posts at suitable intervals,[34] was probably taken to reduce the threat of external intervention and to provide a secure communications corridor between the two bases (cf. Lilybaeum and Gergovia, below). This extension of connecting branch-works also meant that the conversion to a full system of circum/contravallation (as later occurred) could be more readily accomplished.

The experience of operations mounted before Agrigentum may have informed decisions taken at the siege of Lilybaeum. Here, two camps set on either side of the city were linked with field works comprising 'a ditch, a palisade and a wall'.[35] These were subsequently expanded by extending a further set of entrenchments to link the point of attack (where the rams were deployed) with the base-line, ensuring that the forward positions could be reinforced without interruption when required. The success of these arrangements was demonstrated when the entire garrison (strengthened by 10,000 recently arrived reinforcements) was marched out in a dawn attack on the Roman *point d'appui*, but the rapid transfer of reserves to the threatened sector forced the Carthaginians to retreat after sustaining heavy casualties. A more successful enemy sortie was later mounted against the Roman forward positions taking advantage of a furious storm which carried away both the penthouses and the wooden towers which had been sited in advance to provide covering fire for the ram crews. The Roman works and apparatus were set alight and 'the completeness of the destruction was such that the bases of the towers and the posts that supported the battering rams were rendered useless by the fire'.[36] The inability to salvage any equipment in the face of heavy missile fire and the ferocity of the flames, resulted in the decision to abandon the attack in favour of a more passive approach based upon a hermetic investment.

This last episode provides us with our first real details concerning the construction of the Roman extended blockade camp, with the description of the *bracchia* suggesting that considerable attention was paid to defensive capability. The combination of a ditch and a palisade implies a serious effort to establish an obstacle field and the provision of a wall rather than a dump rampart, may have represented an attempt to create a fighting platform from which enemy sorties could be actively resisted. The existence of wooden towers in a forward position at the *point d'appui* is also interesting, with Polybius' statement that the conflagration had rendered their *bases* useless, suggesting that these were earthfast rather than mobile structures.

When Marcellus changed his strategy at Syracuse (214-212 BC), abandoning the hermetic circumvallation in favour of concentrating the army in winter quarters, issues of security may have been uppermost in his mind. With continuing resistance from the defenders of Achradina and 'the Island', and with the Euryalus Fort still holding out behind him, Marcellus pitched camp on open ground within the walls (not wanting his troops to be scattered in the densely built-up area). This position was fortified by bricks taken from demolished buildings.[37] This consolidation of the army in the shelter of a brick-walled camp, continued until the surrender of the isolated Euryalus garrison removed the danger of a direct descent on the Roman rear. Marcellus now ordered that more aggressive approaches be undertaken against the fortified quarter of Achradina, which was blockaded with three carefully sited camps. This continued preference for blockade camps was justifiable given the continuing danger of intervention from Carthaginian expeditionary forces, a threat that crystallized with a concerted (but unsuccessful) attempt mounted against one of these camps.

With the enduring value of the blockade camp demonstrated by the Syracusan campaign, the transition to circumvallatory systems progressed both slowly and inconsistently.

Blockade camps allowed operations to retain a certain flexibility (cf. the example of Carthago Nova, 210 BC, above) enabling commanders to respond to tactical developments without the same expenditure of effort that a re-engineering of a line of investment would involve. This relative adaptability can be readily appreciated during the lengthy siege of Carthage (149-146 BC).

The initial camps established here by Censorinus and Manilius were both vulnerable. The former, pitching camp next to a stagnant lagoon, was forced to relocate to the seashore as his men started to sicken in the unhealthy conditions. His colleague, despite siting his base on the isthmus near to the enemy outworks, provided inadequate defences so that a Carthaginian night attack succeeded in crossing the ditch before the camp and in tearing down stretches of palisade. The near penetration of the base forced Manilius to improve his fortifications by replacing the stake-wall lines with a proper wall [38] and by building a separate fort on the seashore where his supply vessels could be unloaded in security. These various installations were later abandoned.

Upon his assumption of command, Scipio pitched camp at a new location 'not far from Carthage'[39] but still sufficiently distant to allow the defenders to establish their own counter-fort at a range of 5 stades from the walls. This position allowed the defenders to maintain contact with their army of the interior and prevented the Roman blockade from being fully effective. However, the situation again changed following the seizure of the suburb of Megara which forced the defenders to withdraw their extra-mural garrison, leaving Scipio in complete control of the entire isthmus. The order was now given to cut off the landward approaches to the city by means of a trench extending a distance of 25 stades from sea to sea, which was set but 'a spear's cast' from the enemy wall. What might otherwise be thought of as a line of investment was given the character of a blockade camp by a second trench excavated behind but 'at no great distance from the first'[40] facing the hinterland, and by two cross-ditches linking the trenches at their terminal points. All these ditches were filled with sharp stakes and palisades were raised behind them save on the Carthage-facing front, where a wall was built 6ft wide and 12ft high, exclusive of the parapets, and turrets were raised at intervals along its full length. The highest of these turrets, in the middle of the work, was converted into a tower by the addition of four wooden storeys which allowed oversight of the defenders' activities.

These elements took 20 days and nights to construct, the whole army being engaged in either building or in fighting, and the entire force was moved within the completed fortifications. Appian states that this complex acted both as a camp and as a 'long fort' from which supplies sent to the city from the interior could be intercepted, and to this he attributes the principal cause for the famine that eventually gripped the besieged.[41]

It is clear that the construction of this work was carried out in the face of heavy opposition, with the whole army being assigned either to the labour details or to the covering force necessitated by hostile sorties. The proximity of the enemy wall must also have meant that missile fire would have been a serious hindrance, but as other sieges demonstrate (particularly Massilia, 49 BC),[42] extensive construction could still take place in the face of the heaviest barrage provided that adequate screening was provided. However, it was not just enemy missile fire that was feared, as the security measures put in place to protect the encampment readily demonstrate. The basic defensive configuration of a ditch filled with stakes and a palisade line behind, was strengthened on the Carthage-facing front by a wall (presumably brick-built like the one later raised on the quay),[43] of sufficient gauge to have acted as a patrol-walk and fighting platform (as the provision of parapets and turrets at regular intervals confirms). That this was a primarily defensive work is further emphasized by the construction of the observation platform that allowed any enemy build-up to be noted prior to any sally, and by the absence of references to any crossing-point over the ditch, indicating that operations beyond this obstacle were not seriously contemplated. It is also telling that when Scipio did commence offensive approaches, they were undertaken at the harbour, a different front altogether.

Given the proximity of the enemy enceinte, it is likely that the besieged would have been able to overlook the Roman works along their full length, a factor emphasized by the fact that the central tower had to be raised by four storeys in order for the besiegers to see into the city. These considerations suggest that, by this stage, the defenders' complement of artillery (at least of heavier pieces) had been significantly depleted, as otherwise they would have been capable of clearing the Roman parapets and of demolishing the wooden superstructure of the lookout tower. Presumably Scipio was aware of this weakness before ordering that his forward positions be set so close to the enemy.

Although Scipio's 'quadrilateral' may display certain hybrid qualities by resembling both a line of circumvallation and a blockade camp, the prominence ascribed to its role as the army base and as the centre for the active interception of re-supply attempts (presumably by aggressive patrolling), make the latter identification more appropriate.

The form of the elaborate works employed at Carthage was very much a consequence of the local topography; the influence of terrain in determining how blockade camps were constructed can be similarly appreciated at several other sites such as Alexandrium (57 BC) and Gergovia (52 BC). The first of these involved the reduction of an isolated Hasmonaean fortress[44] that crowned the summit of the conical mountain of Qarn el-Sartabeh (*10* and *colour plate 6*). Although the natural strength of the position made an assault impractical, certain outworks were indeed carried by force when Gabinius' army arrived in the vicinity (an action chiefly noted for the decoration awarded to the young Mark Antony). Thereafter, with the bulk of the Roman army being re-deployed for the pacification of Judaea, matters were pressed by blockade pending Gabinius' return. The disposition of Roman forces left behind to maintain the siege must have been almost entirely conditioned by topographical considerations, with the isolation of the summit being achieved by the careful siting of a small number of camps (*11*). It has been claimed[45] that there may have been up to seven of these Roman forts, some of which were linked by dry-stone walling. In all probability however, the Roman design could have been achieved with fewer, well-sited blocking works on the surrounding ridges and on the plateau to the west. Although the proposed blockade system is intriguing, it appears overly elaborate for the circumstances, a consequence perhaps of a too ready assumption that Roman siege strategy required curtain walls to link its constituent blockade camps. It should also be noted that the subsequent re-occupation of Alexandrium as another Herodian palace-fort complex has also served to confuse the archaeological picture and

10 The
Herodian
citadel at
Alexandrium

it is possible that some of the wall-lines shown on Meshel's plan may be connected with this later phase (perhaps relating to water collection for the cisterns?).[46]

At Gergovia the terrain again played an important role in determining the Caesarian siege strategy. As the *oppidum* was sited in a high position with difficult approaches, an assault was considered impractical and a full-scale circumvallation was deemed too risky whilst there was a subsisting threat to the Roman supply lines. Accordingly, Caesar resolved to proceed more cautiously by seizing a subsidiary hill that enjoyed strong natural defences, allowing him to deny access to the principal Gallic water source and to prevent the defenders from foraging at will.[47] This hill was then fortified and linked to the main camp by means of a 'double ditch, 12ft broad in each case ... so that even single soldiers could pass to and fro safe from a sudden onset of the enemy'.[48] It is interesting that Caesar makes explicit reference to the advantage of providing a secure corridor between the two camps reflecting past practice (as seen at Lilybaeum).

In the course of excavations in 1862, Napoleon III's workers uncovered the evidence for this linking work 'which composed a rampart formed by the upcast of two adjoining ditches each having a depth of 4ft and a width of 6ft, so that the width of the two (combined) was no more than 12ft.'[49] Although the dimensions of the ditches do not sound particularly impressive, it must be assumed that the accompanying rampart (comprised of their fill) was provided with a palisade of stakes to afford those in transit some protection from enemy missile fire. There would have been no need to give the corridor more powerful defences as any hostile attack directed against the line would have been countered by legionary deployment out of one or other of the camps. Napoleon III also observes that it would have been faster to excavate two relatively shallow ditches than one large work, and when speed was an important consideration (to forestall any attempt by the defenders to cut off the garrison of the smaller camp), such a design may have suited Caesar's operational plan.

The extended blockade camp at Gergovia was intended to house a complement of six legions (and an unspecified number of auxiliaries) and when Caesar withdrew four of these to confront an Aeduan column, the two remaining legions were hard-pressed to maintain their position as 'there was no time at such a crisis to reduce the camp area.'[50] In the face of determined enemy attacks, the camp garrison made good use of its artillery (presumably including all the army's engines as the troops under Caesar had marched out 'in light order') to defend the ramparts. Once the assaults had ceased for the day, Fabius gave the order for all but two of the camp gates to be barricaded and for screens to be added to the ramparts in preparation for the next day's combat. It is instructive that, despite this pressure, Fabius did not seek to concentrate his forces in one or other of the camps but sought to defend the whole system, which may explain why two gates were left unblocked if they were the ones that gave access to the connecting corridor. The addition of screens to the ramparts would have served to shelter the troops against the Gallic archers who had caused many casualties on that first day.

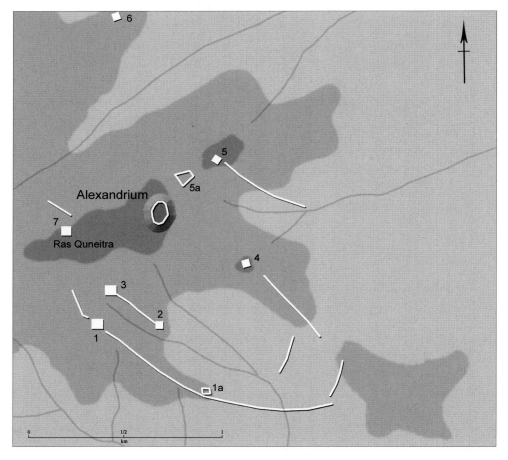

11 The siege system at Alexandrium with possible Roman *castella* (1-7) and the 'blockade walls'. *Suggested by Meshel, 1984*

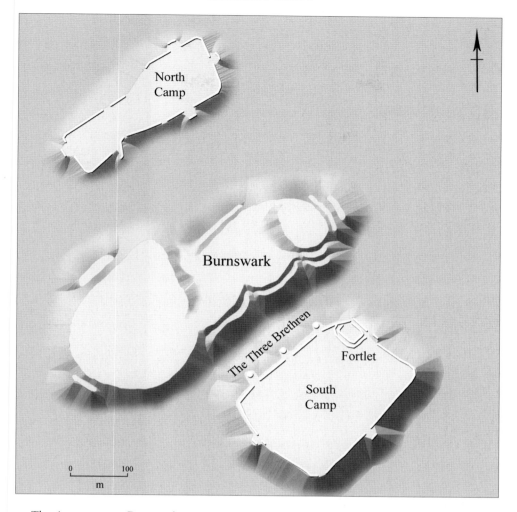

12 The siege system at Burnswark

The crucial importance of artillery in breaking up the Gallic attack on Fabius' understrength garrison may have an interesting bearing on the situation at Burnswark (*12*). Here, two camps established north and south of the hillfort respectively may have represented the bivouacs of separate, converging army columns (cf. Corfinium). The first formation to arrive would have taken up position in the South Camp, a conclusion partly predicated upon the heavy defences provided for the upslope (enemy-facing) front of that encampment. These appear to have comprised a ditch *c.*5.5m wide and 1.8m deep (1.2m of which was cut through bedrock) backed by a rampart 2.8m above the ditch base (*13*).[51] This rampart was sufficiently wide at its base (6.5m) to have acted as a proper fighting platform and the three regularly-spaced gateways driven through it were shielded by reinforced mounds (*14*) up to 3.5m high and 11m to 15m across which have been interpreted as artillery platforms (playing a dual role in disrupting any enemy

13 The north ditch of the South Camp at Burnswark with 'The Three Brethren'

sortie and in providing suppressive fire for any attempted assault).[52] As these traverses are of an entirely different character to those provided in advance of the entrances on the other sides of the camp, and because the northern rampart and ditch are of a substantially greater order of magnitude than the rest of the enceinte, it is reasonable to suppose that these elaborate measures were intended to confront a very real enemy threat. Protected by such works, a besieging commander could have awaited the arrival of his reinforcements with some confidence.

The North Camp, representing the encampment of the second element of the siege army, would have sealed any escape route to the north (15), albeit that this base may not have been completed before the end of the operation. In any event, that the two camps had been sited out of direct line-of-sight of each other would lend credence to the idea that the positions had been linked by some form of connecting work and it is tempting to view Christison & Barbour's 'line of circumvallation'[53] in this light. Although the evidence in support of this hypothesis may be tenuous, with various earthworks of indeterminate date crossing the eastern slopes, the notion that a protected corridor was opened between the two main garrison bases would certainly accord with precedent (16). Therefore, until detailed survey and excavation work can resolve the issue, the possibility that an extended blockade camp system may once have been drawn around the eastern flanks of Burnswark Hill should be recognized.

In terms of archaeological evidence, it is only the two blockade camps at Nahal Hever that can rival Burnswark as a source of information for this type of siege work. We have already seen how these encampments operated in tandem to oversee, and to prevent any escape from, the cliff-face caves that sheltered Jewish insurgents during the Bar Kokhba rebellion, even though this specialist role may limit the comparative value of these sites more generally.

Perched on the cliff-edge, both these camps (*8* and *9*) were defended by relatively flimsy stone walls on their plateau-facing fronts, demonstrating that the possibility of an enemy attack was never seriously contemplated. Also, the limited area that these defences enclosed indicate how economical the blockade camp option could be in terms of manpower (with Yadin estimating[54] that the garrison of camp A would have been in the order of 80-100 men, a total that the slightly smaller camp B is unlikely to have exceeded). Clearly the emphasis in this case was upon surveillance, and the manner in which the two camps were designed to act in conjunction (with cliff-top signalling stations being maintained at both sites) shows how the topography was used to best advantage.

The relatively straightforward form of the works at Nahal Hever serves to remind us that blockade camps were not always complemented by complex branch-works or satellite outposts. Several examples exist of these 'simple' blockade camps, albeit that their occurrence in the sources is usually connected with some form of unfortunate reverse suffered by the besiegers! At Numantia (140 BC), Pompeius Aulus was driven back inside the fortifications of his camp and when he attempted to over-winter, he lost a large number of soldiers due to their 'being exposed to severe cold without shelter'.[55] This lack of proper provision not only indicates the strategic naivety of the commander (who should have withdrawn to friendly territory) but also suggests that the construction of *hibernacula* involved much more careful planning than the siting of a summer base camp.

14 'The Three Brethren' at Burnswark

15 The North Camp at Burnswark

16 Possible earthwork linking the North and South Camps at Burnswark

This latter point was not lost on Metellus, who abandoned the siege of Zama (109 BC?) when the campaigning season came to an end[56] (although this decision may also have been influenced by earlier events at site which demonstrated the potential weakness of the unsupported blockade camp). In this case, whilst Metellus' men were attempting to press ahead with a general assault on the walls in various sectors, Jugurtha fell upon the Roman camp and forced an entry. It was only a desperate last stand that gave Metellus the time to lead a relief column to repel the Numidian king. Thereafter, a cavalry screen was posted to shield the camp whilst the Romans returned to the attack, but the fact that the Numidians managed to ambush this covering force and had to be driven off by the camp guard, suggests that the position remained vulnerable. Such exposure could also occur where the siege system employed a series of unconnected blockade camps, as the Pompeian investment of Salonae (48 BC) makes clear. This pro-Caesarian centre was surrounded by five camps from which the besiegers attempted assaults as well as maintaining the blockade.[57] However, the defenders were able to take advantage of the besiegers' negligence by sallying out at noon (when the attackers had withdrawn into their respective camps) and by attacking each encampment in turn. The entire Pompeian force was routed in detail in the forlorn defence of the individual camps.

Another class of field encampment best treated as a form of blockade camp is the detached fort deployed some distance from the centre under attack so as to break up any external relief attempt. The advanced position fortified by Caesar on the isthmus to the south of Thapsus (46 BC) is a case in point as it prevented any direct advance by Scipio's forces towards the town, allowing the Caesarian forces time to complete their main, crescent-shaped camp before the target.[58] A similar scheme was employed at Ategua (45 BC), where a network of forts were built at tactically advantageous positions beyond the line of investment.[59] Despite their apparent isolation, these outposts managed to hold Gn. Pompeius' field army at arm's length and frustrated his attempts to raise the siege. It is also possible that a system of this nature was also employed at Bethar (AD 135), where fortified positions located up to 4km from the target (colour plate 7) may have been designed to forestall any attempt to disrupt the close investment of Bar Kochba's capital.

The apparent decline in field fortification as an automatic component of Roman campaign manoeuvres would appear to have had a knock-on effect in the prosecution of sieges as well. From the third century AD onwards there are very few accounts which mention pitching camp before a besieged centre, and that Ammianus chooses to lay such emphasis on the process when it does occur, implies that the actions of his protagonists were considered unusual. Thus at Bezabde (AD 360), having undertaken an initial reconnaissance, Constantius is reported to have pitched camp and 'fortified it by a rampart and with deep ditches'.[60] When Julian arrived before Maiozamalcha (AD 363), his first camp was relocated to a more favourable site and was fortified with a double rampart,[61] because of the perceived threat offered by the enemy cavalry. The danger of enemy sorties was forcefully brought home to Julian after heavy casualties were inflicted in the course of a hostile sally by the defenders of his next target, a fort near Ctesiphon. Thereafter, the order was given that the army camp should be protected at all times by a 'rampart or a dense array of stakes and a deep ditch.'[62] That these (not particularly elaborate) defensive measures would have formed part of the conventional repertoire of the army on the march in earlier centuries, suggests either that the whole process of castrametation had become unfamiliar to the soldiers of the later empire or that their usual bivouacs were only ever lightly defended. Whatever the conclusion, there is little evidence to suggest that the blockade camp concept survived the tactical re-orientation that led to the tactics of assault being preferred over indirect approaches.

5

CIRCUMVALLATION

Having discussed the role of blockade camps in the Roman siege system, it is now necessary to consider the other main device for ensuring the isolation of a defended centre: a line of circumvallation.

Circumvallation is treated here as a generic term covering any work of encirclement designed to ensure the complete investment of a target. The emphasis upon a continuous linear barrier distinguishes this type of siege work from the extended blockade camp, although the 'curtain wall' (or other form of connecting obstacle) may only constitute one component of the circumvallatory system. Apart from this general usage, the term also has a specific meaning in the context of any scheme involving two separate lines of investment. Here, *circumvallation* may be taken to refer to the outward-facing barrier, whilst an inward-facing line (confronting the besieged) should be distinguished as a *contravallation*. This distinction will be maintained whenever a double investment system is under discussion, but otherwise examples involving only one encircling line will be identified simply by the generic description of 'circumvallation'.

THE ROMAN USE OF CIRCUMVALLATION

Given that the isolation of a defended centre by means of a continuous barrier was an obvious means of achieving a blockade, the use of this tactic in some of the earliest Roman siege campaigns is predictable (e.g. against Velitrae in the 620s BC and during the second year of the operation mounted against Fidenae, 495 BC).[1] However, doubts over the reliability of our sources in such matters (see chapter 1) and the questionable capability of the armed forces of the early Roman state, raise serious concerns as to whether these early episodes indeed involved the construction of hermetic works of encirclement. After all, raising a line of circumvallation would have involved considerable planning and expertise both in terms of construction and in the organization of the supply and maintenance of the garrison watching over it. Nevertheless, the apparent Roman proficiency in extemporizing field fortifications to trap enemy troops who were themselves engaged in the siege of a fixed target[2] may imply that the skills that allowed the rapid construction of such works had been honed in earlier operations directed against enemy towns. Of course, such early circumvallatory schemes need not have involved complex structures (probably no more than the ditch and palisade that Dionysius of Halicarnassus mentions at Velitrae above), and this relative lack of sophistication makes the elaborate works described before Veii[3] much less likely as a credible contemporary undertaking.

The paucity of references to the use of circumvallation in the century or so following the capture of Veii (with Camillus' initiation of such a scheme at Satricum, 386 BC, providing the only recorded example),[4] may cast further doubt upon the employment of the technique in the preceding period as well. However, as Roman campaigns were now waged at a progressively greater distance from their main centres of population, problems of re-supply and reinforcement may have precluded attempts to isolate towns deep within hostile territory. This is not to say that sieges did not take place, but rather, that the troops engaged in the reduction of distant targets were better served by the blockade camp. The latter offered a secure base and a concentration in the face of the enemy instead of exposing a dispersed garrison to the threat of an overwhelming counter-attack.

The annexation of greater territories and the consequent expansion of available resources fuelled a dramatic increase in the scale and ambition of Roman military adventurism. The First Punic War and the struggle for hegemony in Sicily, saw the regular deployment of large armies (sometimes with a strength in excess of 100,000 men), and with such capacity at their disposal, Roman commanders began to employ circum-vallation with greater frequency. However, this adoption of blockade by encirclement was tempered by caution as the examples of Agrigentum (262 BC), Lilybaeum (250-249 BC) and Syracuse (214-212 BC) readily illustrate.[5]

It was the success of the double ditch and rampart thrown around Capua (212-211 BC) that provided the first real endorsement of the value of a well-organized (and well-garrisoned) circumvallatory scheme.[6] Also, with the Romans facing powerful hostile forces, both within the walls and outside, this episode also marks the first record of the developed double investment system that reached its apogee in the Caesarian lines before Alesia. Although precautions against external interference had previously been taken at Agrigentum, the elaboration here of a full scheme of circum/contravallation (with both sets of ramparts forming proper 'fighting platforms'), meant that Capua could be kept encircled notwithstanding the presence of Hannibal's relief force. This is in marked contrast to Syracuse, where the threat of a Carthaginian field army persuaded Marcellus to abandon his circumvallation in favour of a secure concentration based upon a blockade camp.

Following the Capuan success, there was a marked increase in the use of circum-vallation, even though none of these works (with the possible exception of Orongis, 207 BC)[7] would appear to have been on a particularly impressive scale. For example, the rampart and ditch drawn around Ambracia (189 BC)[8] were insufficient to prevent Aetolian reinforcements from forcing their way into the besieged centre. Furthermore, that the process of circumvallation was still poorly understood by certain commanders is indicated by the success enjoyed by Viriathus when his forces sallied out of Erisana (c.141 BC)[9] routing the Roman troops employed in line construction. Such setbacks suggest that the importance of screening works and covering forces for the protection of the labour details had yet to be appreciated.

The careful preparations[10] made in advance of Scipio's Numantine campaign (134-133 BC) and the elaborate system raised around this hill town (*colour plate 4*),[11] demonstrate that this was one general who appreciated both the functional role of circumvallation and the appropriate form that such works should take. With no appreciable external threat, Scipio was able to concentrate upon the isolation of the defenders whilst simultaneously ensuring the security of his own troops, and the success of his scheme was widely admired by the classical authors.

Although Scipio's strategy at Numantia would presumably have become a familiar anecdote of Roman military achievement, there are only a few sieges subsequent to this in which circumvallation was to play a similarly passive role (notably, the blockade of the Younger Marius in Praeneste, 82 BC or the containment of Lucius Antonius at Perusia, 41-40 BC).[12] Circumvallation, instead, began to be viewed as a useful precursor to more direct approaches, enabling the isolation of the target whilst simultaneously providing a secure base-line from which further offensive measures might be initiated. One of the first examples of this new, aggressive doctrine can be recognized at Metellus' siege of Thala (*c.*108 BC), where the hostile desert environment (and the need to transport water supplies over a 50-mile trail) helped persuade the Roman commander to advance engines and to raise a supporting siege mound as soon as his encirclement had been completed.[13]

Such methods can be recognized as precursors of the standard Caesarian siege approach, whereby assault preparations were put in hand immediately after the circumvallation had been completed (as at the stronghold of the Aduatuci, 57 BC, or Ategua, 45 BC).[14] Indeed, the widely publicized success of these tactics in the Gallic War, may well have persuaded Caesar's contemporaries in other theatres towards emulation, even if such elaboration may not always have been strictly necessary. The methodical manner in which Cicero approached the reduction of the small Cilician town of Pindenissus (51 BC) can be considered a case in point. Here, the learned governor proceeded with a strongly-held line of circumvallation and pushed forward earthworks, penthouses and towers against the walls.[15] That the operation took 57 days to secure a surrender, suggests that the Caesarian example had been poorly understood, with this relatively insignificant target scarcely meriting such elaborate and long, drawn-out preliminaries (even if Cicero's objective had been to secure a 'triumph' rather than to conduct a balanced military campaign).

Alesia (52 BC), however, demonstrates that Caesar did not always treat circumvallation as a preface to the main forward thrust. Gravely outnumbered both by the defenders within the *oppidum* and by the relief forces gathering in his rear, Caesar made no attempt to force the issue by means of assault, concentrating instead upon a blockade secured by a heavily protected circum/contravallation.[16] By forcing the Gauls to attack his positions, and by timely transfers of reserves between the threatened sectors, Caesar was able to overcome his numerical disadvantage, although the enemy's failures of co-ordination and Vercingetorix's passivity whilst the Roman works were being constructed, also contributed to the final outcome.

During the early Principate, although some actions continued to follow the general 'aggressive' pattern (as at Segesta, 35 BC),[17] less direct methods were also employed where appropriate (as in the simple encirclement of the Cantabrian army on Mt Medullus,

26 BC).[18] Perhaps comparative peace in the east combined with the absence of any organized and technically informed opponents in the west, meant that those sieges where isolation preceded assault were no longer regarded as operationally necessary. Any decrease in the use of the technique would also have a direct impact on subsequent campaigns, as the process of field fortification and the efficient raising of structures to facilitate an assault would have depended upon a well-trained workforce. Accordingly, less practice in the field might have resulted in a reduction of the army's capacity to undertake large-scale engineering projects of this nature (at least in any rapidly extemporized sense). Some evidence for this can be seen during the Flavian suppression of the Jewish revolt when the opening stages were marked by an apparent reluctance to engage in any formal circumvallation until the failure of direct approaches compelled a re-evaluation of strategy (e.g. at Iotapata, AD 67 and Jerusalem, AD 70). However, by the time the Tenth legion was detailed to complete the elimination of the surviving centres of resistance after the fall of Jerusalem, its veterans had acquired sufficient expertise to be able to press ahead with technically proficient and well-sited lines of investment, not to mention assault ramps that were every bit as ambitious as any raised by Caesar's experienced troops.[19]

The lack of operational detail contained in the accounts of most sieges conducted after this period prevents any proper assessment of the declining use of circumvallation by later commanders. Presumably this can again be related to the relative infrequency of 'city-taking' campaigns resulting in an erosion of the hard-won experiences of the past, and the substitution of immediate strategies of assault over more methodical preparations. It should be noted that one of the few occasions for which we have definite archaeological evidence for the employment of circumvallation (the siege of Bethar, AD 135)[20] came at the close of the second Jewish revolt (17 and *colour plate 8*), another arduous pacification involving a series of set-piece blockades to achieve its final objective. We can probably assume that protracted episodes such as the epic reduction of Byzantium (AD 194-196) would also have involved the construction of circumvallatory systems (at least, to cut off the landward approaches in this instance), although our sources remain silent in this regard.[21]

Apart from the remains at Hatra (which are better viewed as Sassanian works),[22] the only site of the later Empire with unequivocal evidence for the use of circumvallation is Cremna (AD 277-278).[23] However, Zosimus' relatively generous account of this operation does not refer to the circum/contravallatory system employed here (*colour plate 9*), raising the possibility that accounts of other sieges are similarly flawed. Also, the specific topography of this site and the aim of the operation to neutralize a nexus of revolt may have acted to confer a unique character to the reductive approach adopted in any event.

Notwithstanding this uncertainty surrounding the employment of circumvallation in the third century, there can be little doubt as to its redundancy by the mid-fourth century. In the detailed treatment that Ammianus Marcellinus affords various sieges in the east, there is no indication of any attempt to surround a target with anything more than a simple cordon of troops. Vegetius, too, alludes[24] to the archaic practice of encircling a target with a breastwork, reinforcing the impression that circumvallation had been abandoned as a serious tactic of siege warfare. This outcome can be ascribed to the dominance of assault strategies, with the preference for more direct methods of attack

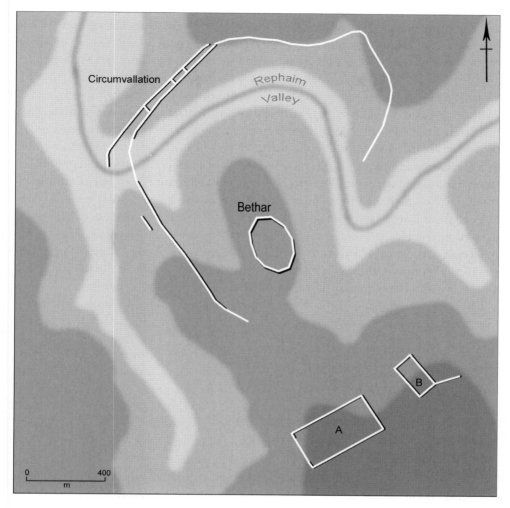

17 The siege system at Bethar. *After Ussishkin 1993*

perhaps dictated by unit size reductions in the later Empire. Smaller formations may not have enjoyed sufficient critical mass to engage in large-scale field fortification, and the seeming failure to engage in temporary camp construction when on the march[25] would have given such units scarce experience of the necessary engineering techniques, even when they were aggregated together to form large armies.

FORM AND STRUCTURE

The isolation of a target by continuous field works can be achieved in many ways and the precise configuration of any given system depends upon several factors. These include the nature of the terrain, the raw materials locally available, the troop strengths of besieger and besieged, the experience and foresight of the besieging commander, and the exigencies of the general military situation. Although many of these issues are addressed in chapter 2, their impact upon the decision to proceed with the construction of a circumvallatory scheme (and the way in which they might determine the physical form of the resulting works) should be acknowledged here.

We will now concentrate upon the structural attributes of the circumvallation starting with a consideration of its most important element:

(a) The continuous linear barrier

Although blockade camps might be connected by linking works of varying degrees of elaboration, a true system of circumvallation can be recognized from the manner in which it completely isolates the target from its hinterland via a continuous linear barrier. It is this hermetic quality that is the essence of circumvallation, and although in rare cases[26] the works may still have been incomplete at the time of surrender, the suggestion that some systems would have been designed with an 'open' side (as Zertal suggests for Narbata)[27] makes little tactical sense. After all, if the decision had been taken to isolate a target, then it would be difficult to understand why the resulting scheme would be compromised by leaving a gaping hole in the course of the line. The different forms of barrier will now be discussed.

(i) The simple ditch and the ditch and palisade

The easiest way to seal off a site is to excavate a ditch around it, which, with the addition of some form of stockade behind, should prove sufficient to prevent easy access to or egress from the target. Thus the earliest circumvallation recorded in our sources is that mentioned by Dionysius of Halicarnassus at Velitrae, which he reports as being surrounded with a ditch and palisades. Similar obstacles are also cited by the same source at both Fidenae and at Antium (459 BC).[28] Although the construction of such barriers would not have posed much of a technical challenge, the organizational impetus that could have arranged the manning of the same is more believable in a fifth- rather than a seventh-century context.

This relatively simple form of encirclement was also used more ambitiously at Agrigentum (262 BC) where two sets of trenches were dug, both to protect against sallies from the city and to thwart any external relief attempt. Fortified posts were also added at intervals along the lines by way of reinforcement.[29] This, our first example of a dual system of circum/contravallation, proved its worth by successfully repulsing a simultaneous attack. However, this outcome can probably be attributed to a forewarning received by the besiegers rather than any intrinsic strength of the works, as a part of the Carthaginian garrison subsequently managed to escape in a night-time sortie.[30] At Lilybaeum (250-241 BC), the ditch that was dug to surround the city after the failure of direct approaches was strengthened by a palisade in contrast to the wall that was simultaneously built around the Roman encampment.[31] The greater care taken over the defences of their base suggests that the besiegers did not regard the circumvallation as a defensible line, rather, that their ring-work was simply designed as an obstacle to enemy movement.

Despite their comparatively unsophisticated forms, the use of the ditch or ditch-palisade combination was not restricted to early Republican warfare. On the contrary, the longevity of their employment can be noted from their appearance at Athens (87–86 BC), Pitane (85 BC), Tigranocerta (69 BC), Segesta (35 BC) and at Mt Medullus (26 BC).[32] It may well be significant that for the first two examples, the stated purpose of the circumvallation was to prevent any escape, whilst the function of the lengthy ditch (of 15,000ft/18 miles, Orosius/Florus) drawn around Mt Medullus was to trap those Cantabrian forces that had sought refuge there. It seems that a simple ditch was considered an adequate measure to achieve this objective in each of these cases. At Tigranocerta and Segesta however, the ditch and the ditch and palisades that surrounded the respective targets, would seem to have been viewed as preliminary stages to the launching of more direct approaches against the enemy walls (i.e. the institution of 'aggressive' circumvallation in the sense previously outlined). The success of the Armenian cavalry in breaking through the encirclement at the former site, serves to illustrate how a simple ditch might not prove sufficient to contain a determined opponent.

Clearly, the excavation of a continuous ditch would depend upon favourable soil conditions, as the feature would have to be sufficiently wide and deep to form a respectable obstacle. Accordingly, this type of encirclement should not be expected in hilly areas or wherever the bedrock is too close to the surface to allow anything more than a shallow scrape. In such terrain the construction of an alternative form of obstacle might accordingly be expected (although Mt Medullus suggests that this need not always have been the case). Furthermore, if palisades are to be employed as an integral part of the design, then an adequate supply of timber will also be required (as Diodorus Siculus makes explicit for the investment of Panormus, 254 BC, by a palisade and trench running from sea to sea).[33] Of course, any local shortage of timber could be rectified by transportation, although this solution would only be practicable for a considerable logistical establishment operating over secured supply corridors.

(ii) The rampart and the rampart and ditch

The most commonly encountered formula in the classical accounts of circumvallatory works is that they comprised a *vallum fossaque* (rampart and ditch), although the stand-alone 'rampart' or 'wall' is almost as frequently described. These variants are the only types of circumvallation that have been recorded archaeologically.

The *vallum* may take various forms ranging from a straightforward dump rampart built up from the soil excavated whilst digging the ditch(es), to more complex earthen structures revetted with timber, turf or stone and/or strengthened by some internal timbering or stone ribbing. It may also appear as a stone wall, usually with large blocks on the outer faces retaining a rubble or a rubble and earth core. This latter form is particularly common in areas with only a thin soil cover and where easily quarried rock outcrops are available.

The first mention of a circumvallation involving the raising of some form of rampart comes during the siege of Fidenae (436–435 BC) and although there are few details as to the precise nature of this work, Livy makes no mention of any supporting ditch suggesting that this may have been a simple stone-built wall.[34] A rampart and ditch was seemingly thrown around Anxur (400-399 BC), whilst the rampart employed by Camillus at Satricum (386 BC) was likely to have been of the dump variety as there was enough soil in the vicinity to allow for the simultaneous advance of an *agger*.[35] At Orongis (207 BC), a more complex version was deployed comprising a ditch and double rampart which may be reconstructed either as a circum/contravallation or as a reinforced line facing the enemy town.[36] The latter explanation should perhaps be preferred given that L. Scipio was confronted by numerous defenders, albeit that the layout of the resulting system must remain conjectural.

If it was considered likely that the defenders (or a relief force) might mount a serious attack on the encirclement, then measures would have to be taken to reinforce the defensive value of the barrier, converting the same from a simple obstacle to a proper 'fighting platform'. This was clearly the case at Capua (212-211 BC) where the construction of double ditches and ramparts was part of the carefully planned investment.[37] Many factors persuade us to regard this as a proper system of circum/contravallation: the threat posed by Hannibal's relief army; that there was sufficient space for the army to camp in the interval between the two walls; and that the two consuls apportioned the responsibility for holding each line separately between themselves. The formidable nature of the works is indicated by the ease with which Appius Claudius repulsed the Campanians from the 'inner' rampart, and although Hannibal's troops succeeded in penetrating the 'outer' line, the effort left them in sufficient disarray to be swept aside in a counter-attack. It is clear that the Romans engaged the enemy directly from their ramparts which were equipped with battlements[38] to improve their defensible qualities.

The Scipionic reduction of Numantia (134-133 BC) was also preceded by the construction of a circumvallation designed to withstand determined attack, consisting of a wall '8ft wide and 10ft high, exclusive of the parapets' which was fronted by a ditch set with palisades.[39] Although no trace has been found of this forward ditch, the archaeological investigation of Scipio's barrier has demonstrated the powerful nature of the main construction (*18*). The base of the circumvallation had an average width of 4m (although this varied significantly between 2.4m-6m in different sectors) and the excavator sought to explain this discrepancy with the reported dimensions by claiming that Appian's measurement referred to the width of the parapet walk.[40] Scipio's standing instructions for the prosecution of the campaign (with 20,000 men being detailed to man the wall-top and with 10,000 men being held in immediate reserve),[41] prove that his intention was to maintain an effective defensible cordon at all times. In the circumstances, it is not surprising to note that the barrier was constructed on such a substantial scale, and the addition of a unique central stone 'spine' (*19*) was presumably intended as a further buttress to improve the stability of the rubble and earth fill of the rampart.

Other circumvallatory schemes in which the besieger adopted a defensive stance in the face of a dangerous enemy also involved elaborate engineering provision. Thus when Crassus trapped Spartacus in the mountains south of Thurii (71 BC), he isolated his opponent with a ditch 15ft wide and deep, a palisade and a wall 'of astonishing height and strength'.[42] This system proved effective in repulsing Spartacus' attempts to

Above: 18 The
circumvallation at
Numantia heading
downhill from Dehesilla

Right: 19 The 'three-
ribbed' circumvallation
north of Pena Redonda at
Numantia

break out until he escaped under the cover of a blizzard. Again, when Octavian had cornered Lucius Antonius at Perusia (41-40 BC), his initial encirclement of the town with an extensive ditch and palisade perimeter was considered inadequate to confront the joint threat of Ventidius' relief force and the aggressive stance taken by the besieged. Accordingly, Octavian gave orders to convert his line into a more formidable work by extending the ditch until it measured 30ft in depth and width and raising a wall and providing it with a timber superstructure, not to mention building 'every other kind of entrenchment with double front'.[43] It is not clear what form was taken by the externally-facing defences, although the reference to these supplementary entrenchments suggests that no continuous rampart was built to face the Umbrian countryside (unless ditches were dug to connect a series of detached forts). In any event, Ventidius made no serious effort to interfere with the operation. Lucius Antonius, on the other hand, faced with the real danger of famine, made careful preparations for a simultaneous assault on the contravallation on several fronts, and manufactured easy-to-assemble 'folding towers' that could be moved up to allow his men access to the wall-top.[44] Despite filling in the ditch, breaking down the palisades and mounting the wall in places, the besieged were ultimately forced back by sheer weight of numbers. This near success prompted Octavian to order that reserves be posted close up behind the barrier and his troops trained to man the parapets at speed (presumably to reinforce the permanent watch).[45]

The ultimate expression of a circumvallatory system intended to offer protection to the besiegers whilst maintaining a tight blockade of the enemy, was that instituted by Caesar at Alesia. Although this was not the monolithic set of works that is implied in the *de Bello Gallico*,[46] with each sector receiving a different suite of defences depending upon the level of the perceived threat, the ensemble nonetheless amounts to the most powerful set of field entrenchments known from the Roman world. The most comprehensive measures were provided for the plaine des Laumes (*20*), where the contravallation comprised two outer ditches (one of which was water-filled for much of its course), an obstacle-strewn (at least in part) *glacis*, and a third trench backed by a turf-revetted rampart *c.*5m wide. Facing the opposite direction and over 100m to the rear of the rampart of the contravallation, was the line of circumvallation. This comprised an advanced obstacle field, a double ditch (the outermost again being flooded over much of its length) separated by a *glacis* (with some traces of supplementary obstacles) and a rampart, possibly up to 7m wide. The whole system was designed to delay an attacker sufficiently to allow the deployment of reserves to reinforce the threatened sector, with the depth of the defended zone allowing the turret-mounted artillery to inflict maximum casualties as the enemy's momentum was checked by the outer defences.

The modern excavations undertaken at Alesia[47] have given us some idea of the diversity in the form of Roman ditches and allow us to evaluate the accuracy of frequently encountered statements in the sources that features were dug 'to an equal depth and width'. The three ditches of the contravallation may be taken as examples. The outermost (Ditch 1)[48] varied significantly in width (4m-6.5m) although it possessed a more uniform depth (1.25m-1.5m); the second ditch[49] had a consistent width (2.7m) and a broadly comparable depth (1.1m-1.5m); Ditch 3[50] was the least regular, with a

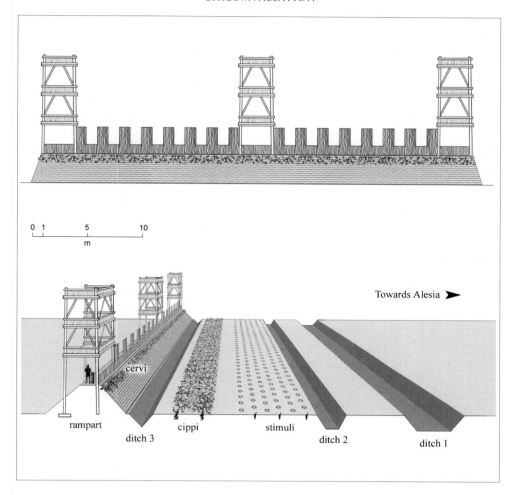

0 1   5   10
     m

Towards Alesia ➤

cervi

rampart   cippi   stimuli

ditch 3   ditch 2   ditch 1

20 Representation of the contravallation and obstacle field on the plaine des Laumes, Alesia

fluctuating width (1.1m–3.2m) and depth (0.8m–1.4m). In all cases, the profiles of these features smoothed out from a pronounced v-shape to a more flattened u-shape the further south they ran (Ditch 1 becoming fully trough-shaped, with a 3m-wide flat base, allowing it to serve as a moat). As the alluvial soil of the plaine des Laumes provides a homogenous background, these variations must reflect the application of differential digging techniques. In all probability, the discrepancies indicate the industry (or competence) demonstrated by separate work-gangs labouring within the framework of a general set of instructions. The parameters of these instructions may have been subject to local interpretation except where there was careful monitoring (the uniformity in the width of Ditch 2 may have resulted from the precise demarcation of this feature by the responsible engineer). Such variations (particularly apparent in the 'practice works' at Woden Law; *21*)[51] suggest that ditch dimensions may not have been as regular and tidy as our sources might otherwise indicate.

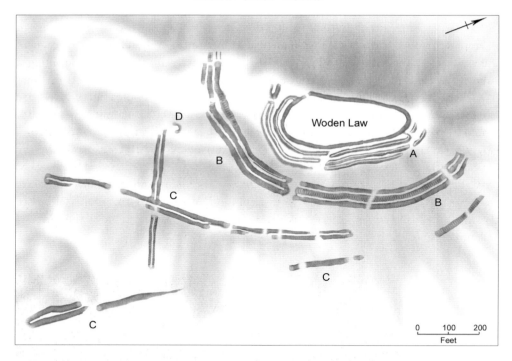

21 Roman practice works at Woden Law with hillfort defences (A), Roman double ramparts in discontinuous sections (B), secondary single rampart lines (C) and putative artillery base (D). *After RCAHMS 1956*

It is also interesting that in less threatened sectors, economies of labour appear to have been applied, again suggesting exaggeration in claims of uniformity. For example, on the montagne de Bussy, where the circumvallation approached camp C the (single) ditch was scarcely a credible obstacle being only 0.3m-0.6m deep.[52] However, this may not have been apparent to any potential assailant as a dense entanglement of *cippi* would have prevented any reconnaissance party from making a detailed observation of the ditch.

The impressive scale of the excavated works at Alesia and Numantia reflect systems built under exceptional circumstances, where even large Roman armies required artificial defences to protect them from dangerous enemies. In contrast, the usual siege scenario did not require such elaborate provision and the works of containment were built to a more modest standard. Although probably a result of their location in hilly or inhospitable terrain, all but one of the surviving corpus of circumvallatory works that fall within this 'simpler' category are of the stand-alone stone wall variety. The exception is the site of Corfinium (49 BC), where the circumvallation (to the east of the town, at any rate) would appear to have consisted of a deliberately scarped hillslope (giving a vertical advantage of *c.*1.5m) fronted by a ditch (*22*). It is likely nonetheless, that the material derived from these labours was piled up to form a rampart along the crest of the resulting 'terrace'. Much more typical however, are the circuits provided at Narbata (AD 66?), Machaerus (AD 72), Masada (AD 73), Bethar (AD 135) and Cremna (AD 277-278).

These sites all feature stone-built walls without supporting ditches, where the terrain is employed instead to derive maximum tactical advantage. The character of each of these walls is remarkably similar, with larger facing stones front and back retaining a rubble core (*23*). At Narbata (*colour plate 10*) and Cremna, where sections across the lines have been obtained, shallow foundation trenches preceded wall construction, with large stones laid at the bottom of the same acting as basal courses. The consistency in width shared by these wall lines should also be noted: the widest on average is that of Narbata (*24*), where the recorded dimensions of 2.15m-2.2m were recovered by excavation;[53] the contravallation at Cremna is 1.8m-2m wide[54] as is most of the circuit at Machaerus[55] (save for a reinforced section of 2.4m at the point most open to attack);[56] that at Masada is 1.5m-1.8m.[57] The wall at Bethar (*25*) is significantly narrower at 1m-1.5m[58] (although the quality of data in respect of this site is significantly weaker), whilst the circumvallation at Cremna barely attains 1m for much of its course.

22 The circumvallation at Narbata descending the Wadi el-Jiz

23 Circumvallation east of Corfinium

24 The western
circumvallation at
Narbata

25 The
circumvallation (A)
on the ridge west
of Bethar with a
secondary wall (B)
running parallel to it

26 Eroded section
of the eastern
circumvallation at
Masada showing
the facing blocks
front and rear and
rubble fill

The significance of these dimensions lies in what they tell us about the width required for the provision of a patrol walk along the wall top. Such a *chemin des rondes* would have been essential for ensuring the proper surveillance of the system, and for providing a platform (albeit a constricted one) for resisting enemy attempts to cross the linear barrier. It should probably be assumed that this patrol walk would have been shielded by some form of parapet, although this would necessarily have involved a reduction in the fighting space along the wall top. Given the measurements that we have, it would seem reasonable to conjecture that a wall gauge of *c.*1.5m would have been the minimum effective width for this sort of barrier, and where narrower dimensions occur, it seems likely that such walls were only ever intended to act as passive obstacles. Certainly, the interpretation of the relatively feeble circumvallation at Cremna as a simple barrier would accord well with the limited provision of supporting turrets along its length (cf. the contravallation at the same site), and probably indicates the limited nature of the perceived external threat.[59]

Although stretches of circumvallation have survived in relatively good order at several sites (particularly along the eastern sector at Masada, *26*), no examples are preserved up to their full, original height. Accordingly, various attempts have been made to ascertain this from the amount of collapse scattered in the vicinity resulting in estimates for the heights of the contravallations at Cremna and Narbata of 2m–2.5m and *c.*3m for Masada.[60] In view of the shortage of timber in these various localities, it is unrealistic to think in terms of an extensive timber superstructure crowning these walls, so that their height, although not much less than the reported 12ft rampart at Alesia[61] and the 10ft rampart at Numantia,[62] would have presented a significantly less impressive aspect given the absence of supplementary breastworks and/or parapets. However, the use of topography to enhance height was a conscious part of the design process at these sites and the walls were laid out with natural gullies to their fore or ran along ridge crests and hill terraces. Thus, even though direct defensibility may not have been the most important functional aspect of these stand-alone stone walls, the engineers responsible for their construction did not miss the opportunity to utilize advantageous local terrain wherever it was expedient to do so.

Before discussing the various supplementary measures that might be undertaken to strengthen a line of circumvallation, we should mention the anomalous case of the encirclement at Hatra. Although this structure may, in places, have resembled some of the other examples (having a part-laid rough stone foundation course), its curious 'casemate-style' of construction has no obvious Roman parallel.[63] This comprised a reinforced stone front, 1.5m thick facing the city with a second, 0.5m thick stone course running *c.*1m behind the first.[64] Both alignments were joined together by 0.5m-thick transversal walls, with each resulting 'compartment' being filled with rubble or mud-brick (*27*). Such elaborate bracing techniques suggest that this structure was intended as a serious fighting platform, although the alien character of the design (not to mention the short duration of the Roman campaigns directed against the city) makes its identification as a Sassanian siege work more plausible.

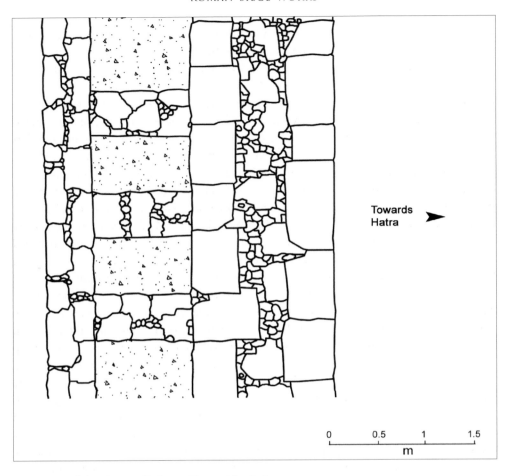

Towards
Hatra

| 0 | 0.5 | 1 | 1.5 |

m

27 Section of the circumvallation at Hatra. *After Andrae 1912*

(iii) Supplementary measures of reinforcement

As we have already noted, the linear barrier could be strengthened by the addition of further obstacles set either in advance of, or between, any of its constituent elements. The Caesarian account of the *lilia*, *stimuli* and *cippi* (see glossary) deployed at Alesia is well known,[65] and excavation has revealed plausible traces of these various devices (even if they are not laid out exactly as described in the text – see *1*). Cone-shaped man-traps identified as *lilia* were located in advance of the outer ditch of the circumvallation on the plaine des Laumes,[66] on the *glacis* between its two ditches on the plaine de Grésigny[67] and in advance of the probable contravallation at the foot of Mont Réa.[68] The best preserved of these survived as shallow pits laid out in a quincunx formation (the symbol for the number 5 on dice), 0.4m–0.5m wide and up to 0.56m deep, with flattened bases *c.*0.3m wide into which stakes would have been driven. Of course, the erosion of the top soil prevents any accurate assessment of the actual depth of these pits at the time of their construction. Gravel patches of slighter character, 0.14m–0.3m wide (some of which evidenced post-pipes for wooden spikes no more than 5cm in diameter), were also located both on the contravallation (behind Ditch 2 on the plaine des Laumes)[69] and on the circumvallation (in advance of the outer ditch, in the same sector).[70] Reasonably enough, these have been taken to represent the Caesarian *stimuli* (although none of the iron barbs crowning the wooden spikes have been found in the modern excavations). Their distribution in a careful quincunx pattern, six rows deep, bears resemblance to a well-ordered *chevaux-de-frise*. As for the *cippi*, shallow, narrow slots in several areas (particularly, in advance of the circumvallation on the montagne de Bussy and on the plaine de Grésigny)[71] have been interpreted as the bedding trenches for these entanglements of sharpened branches. Also, the favourable geology of the montagne de Bussy has allowed the identification of the anchor points for their retaining stakes.

These various measures were designed to impede any enemy attack on the line of encirclement, but if they proved unavailing and the defensive cordon was penetrated in any strength, then the whole siege system might be compromised. As a result, the Caesarian works at Alesia incorporated a (so far) unique mechanism to limit the impact of any local breach and to prevent the further exploitation of an initial Gallic success. This counter-measure (only found on the vulnerable, open terrain of the plaine des Laumes) took the form of a 'bulkhead' across the *intervallum* between the contravallation and the circumvallation.[72] This comprised a cross-ditch 3.8m wide and 1.1m deep (Ditch 5) running across the open ground with a rampart built along its northern edge. A comparable feature (Ditch 6) was located by air photography 123m further to the west, with a rampart on this occasion set along its southern edge. Accordingly, with complementary south-east and north-west facing defences, Ditches 5 and 6 delimited a separate fortified area blocking the *intervallum*. Not only could this have acted as a redoubt where Roman troops might have regrouped following any hostile penetration, it could also have prevented Gallic raiders who had broken into the system from ranging at will behind the Roman lines. It will be interesting to see whether any evidence for a similar 'bulkhead' defensive scheme will be discovered elsewhere in the future.

(iv) Turrets and artillery positions
Features much more commonly encountered in circumvallatory systems are emplacements for artillery which, depending on the circumstances, would have been capable of combining both defensive and offensive roles. Generally, a timber turret or tower emplaced directly on top of a rampart line would have provided adequate support for light, anti-personnel engines intended to break up any attack on the circumvallation itself. Meanwhile, the provision of a reinforced platform (usually immediately behind the line), might suggest more aggressive intent, with the use of heavier machines capable of clearing the enemy parapets or even of inflicting direct structural damage.

The obvious advantages to be secured by raising turrets along the line of the circum-vallation probably meant that their appearance would have predated their first recorded use at the siege of Capua.[73] Their successful contribution to protecting the blockade camp at Carthage[74] presumably would have encouraged Scipio to ensure that his encirclement of Numantia was similarly strengthened, with turrets provided here at intervals of

28 Probable site of Caesarian artillery positions north of the Ategua defences

100ft.[75] Similar close-spacing was recorded at Alesia (every 80ft)[76] and at Perusia (with 1,500 turrets set every 60ft).[77] The violent artillery exchanges that took place at Ategua (45 BC) resulted in one of the Caesarian towers being damaged from its base right up to the third storey,[78] although because the defenders were subsequently able to fire this same structure, it is likely that it comprised part of the superstructure raised on the assault ramp rather than a turret on the more distant line of circumvallation. During the same siege, one of the Pompeian towers (probably a wooden structure raised on the reinforced town wall) was completely demolished and its five-man crew killed, by a single hit from a Caesarian stone-thrower,[79] discharged, presumably, from emplacements on the opposite hill (*28*). Although heavy ploughing has removed any indication of these particular artillery positions at Ategua, there is extensive archaeological evidence for similar structures elsewhere.

Some of the best information regarding turrets on the line of the rampart can be obtained from Alesia. Here, on the most heavily fortified section (the contravallation on the plaine des Laumes), turrets were placed at 15m intervals (i.e. every 50ft instead of the Caesarian 80ft), with rear post-holes significantly deeper than those at the front, suggesting that the two back posts were free-standing whilst the two at the front were partly supported by the fill of the rampart.[80] The approximate dimensions of these structures at 3m x 3m would have been adequate to provide the manoeuvring space for a light catapult. However, this degree of provision was not replicated throughout the Alesian system. On the contravallation on the plaine de Grésigny, although the interval between turrets would appear to have been the same, there is only evidence for two- and not four-post structures. This has led to the suggestion[81] that the front posts of these turrets were sunk into, and supported entirely by, the rampart fill, making them significantly less stable structures than their counterparts on the plaine des Laumes. Elsewhere, the intervals between the turrets vary from 17m-17.5m for the circumvallation on the plaine des Laumes,[82] up to an estimated 60m for the less exposed sector crossing the montagne de Bussy.[83]

Apart from evidence for the addition of turrets to the circumvallation at Numantia (particularly in the Duero-Dehesilla sector where the structures would appear to have had dimensions of 4m x 5m),[84] there are also indications for the use of heavier calibre artillery than light, tower-mounted pieces. This evidence comes in the form of platforms annexed to the rear of the camp ramparts at both Castillejo and Peña Redonda.[85] These appear to have been simple room-like structures that were filled with rubble and earth (and presumably close-boarded) to absorb the recoil shock from heavy engines. The provision of heavy artillery on the northern (externally-facing) rampart of Castillejo cannot be easily explained in view of Scipio's prior overawing of the Numantine allies, but the battery sited on the north-west perimeter of Peña Redonda would have made an enemy attack against the north gate of that camp a costly affair.

The siege works at both Machaerus and Masada were also reinforced with artillery positions, although their character was significantly different to the turrets at Alesia and Numantia because of the stone-built nature of both lines of circumvallation. The examples at Masada (*colour plate 11*) present a relatively homogenous appearance, comprising solid stone-faced and rubble-filled platforms that lie astride the circumvallation,[86] projecting *c.*1m-2m both in front of and behind the wall line, giving a total depth of *c.*5m over a frontage of *c.*4m (*29* and *30*). There is no need to suppose that these turrets were crowned with significant superstructures or that they extended much above the general height of the wall itself, as their defensive function would not have been significantly enhanced by any height advantage. Of the 15 turrets identified on the circuit, 10 are distributed at intervals of *c.*80m-100m along the plain beneath the sheer eastern cliffs, providing reinforcement for a section of line that enjoyed little in the way of natural advantage. Another two examples were intended to provide flanking fire into the Wadi Sebbe (a third covered the crossing of the wadi bottom) and another two performed a similar function for the Wadi Nimre. It is possible that these last positions may also have had a subsidiary role in interdicting access to the lower cisterns on the north-west flanks of the citadel. Despite these turrets having such a robust appearance, there would have been little point in their mounting anything other than light, anti-personnel devices as (apart from the possibly expanded role of the two positions above the Wadi Nimre) the enemy defences would have been out of range. However, there is the possibility that the knoll at the base of the Λευκη may once have accommodated a heavy battery to cover the work on the assault ramp,[87] although the visible evidence is too tenuous to make this suggestion anything more than conjectural.

Above: 29 Turret 11 on the
eastern circumvallation at
Masada

Left: 30 Turret 13 abutting
the eastern circumvallation at
Masada

At Machaerus (*colour plate 12*), a somewhat different solution was adopted to the problem of accommodating the supporting artillery. Along the crest of the southern ridge, 10 small turrets (*31*) were annexed to the back of the circumvallation, eight of which were spaced at 25m–40m intervals between camps C and D, with a further two sited (much farther apart) between camps B and C. These are far slighter than the turrets at Masada, having an average depth behind the wall of only 2m and a frontage of 4m (with the smallest example being 1.8m x 3m).[88] Clearly, if there was to have been sufficient room to mount even the lightest catapult, then the full width of the circum-vallation would have been used as part of the firing platform. This, combined with the lack of any appreciable rubble scatter denoting any significant superstructure, suggests that each 'turret' formed nothing more than an open expansion to the wall top. In all probability, the purpose of these firing stations was not to discourage a direct attack on the circumvallation itself (its ridge-top position would have made such a venture difficult enough),[89] but was to flank any attempt to escape along the bed of the southern Wadi el-Mišneqa. In order to strengthen the point at which the circumvallation crossed this valley (where the enemy were most likely to try and force the line), two artillery platforms were inserted at camp E (involving considerable labour to provide the strong revetment necessary to form stable positions on a steep slope). Opposite these, at camp F, a large stone mound can be taken to represent the setting for another heavy catapult (*colour plate 13 & 32*). Presumably, the care taken over these reinforced emplacements reflected concerns over a mass attack in this sector which heavy artillery would have been useful in breaking up.

31 'Expansion' behind the circumvallation on the ridge south of Machaerus

32 Camp F at Machaerus with heavy artillery stand arrowed

The situation at Cremna is different again. Here, although light pieces could have been placed on the small signal relay turrets set on prominent hillocks immediately behind the course of the contravallation, other stone piles directly on the curtain between turrets 5 and 6, may have formed stations for catapults to provide covering fire for the construction of the siege mound. More significantly, the extensive rubble scatters that adjoin turret 4, where the contravallation projects out like a bastion, suggest that this area may have acted as an artillery base (*colour plate 3*). From here, suppressive fire against the enemy parapets may have been supplemented by a direct bombardment intended to inflict actual structural damage.[90] This would have required the use of heavy weapons, but the visible impact damage to towers 9 and 10 of the town enceinte (and the complete destruction of the front face of a possible forward defensive work sited directly opposite) may well support such a hypothesis.[91]

Although considerable controversy surrounds the formal designation of mounds and platforms as *ballistaria*,[92] it should be quite clear that the repeated and accurate discharge of anything more than a light bolt-firer, would have required the construction of a purpose-built battery. Such a structure needed to have been sufficiently stable to absorb the shock of recoil and sufficiently spacious to allow the proper operation of the artillery piece, both in terms of traversing and elevating. Although the requisite combination might be achieved by several building techniques (with Ammianus suggesting that *onagri* had to be placed in towers made of sun-dried brick or turf, as stone-built examples would have been vulnerable to the concussive shock of discharge),[93] the basic necessity was to provide a platform resting on a stable base. Field work might be expected to recognize

33 Artillery position on the circumvallation at Corfinium

such features, particularly if there are cogent topographical reasons for supporting the identification (as in the case of the artillery position identified on the eastern front at Corfinium, *33*).[94] What appears to be a representation of an artillery position can be seen on Trajan's column[95] where a light *ballista* is mounted on a carefully-built log platform. The ingenious suggestion that this represents an 'exploded diagram' of a forward-sited 'pill-box'[96] may reduce the comparative value of the relief, however.

(b) Camps and strongpoints along the line

The provision of turrets and/or artillery platforms would not have formed the only structural additions to reinforce a line of investment. Even more important would have been the siting of camps to accommodate the garrison manning the system and, where there was an extensive circuit, the establishment of smaller interval forts to act as police posts and as local defence centres. Although our sources sometimes draw a distinction between these two types of fortification (e.g. *castra* contra *castella*), the idiosyncrasies of individual siege actions prevent us from making overly ambitious cross-site comparisons (for example, *castellum* 18 at Alesia has an area of *c*.1.5ha whilst camp H, the largest at Machaerus, is restricted to just 0.19ha). Some basic analysis is nonetheless possible.

(i) Garrison camps

The protracted nature of blockade operations would have meant that the troops would have required adequate accommodation. Accordingly, unless the system of circum/contra-vallation could double up as a *de facto* encampment (as at Capua),[97] the establishment of

34 Camps
F1 and F2 at
Masada with
circumvallation
in front

a secure garrison camp(s) would have been an initial priority. We have already noted the importance of entrenching a defensible camp as part of initial preparatory procedures and these first fortifications were often retained, becoming incorporated within the overall system of investment. Thus Caesar's first camp at Corfinium became the base point from which the line of circumvallation was extended around the town.[98] Similarly, the fortification on Castillejo, established upon Scipio's arrival before Numantia,[99] kept its headquarters function throughout the operation because of its tactically advantageous site. However, it should also be pointed out that changes in the underlying strategy might also result in the abandonment of such positions, as Titus' decision to transfer his base from Mt Scopus to the north-western suburbs of Jerusalem demonstrates.[100]

Large garrison camps ensured that sufficient men could be securely quartered in proximity to the line of works that they were meant to hold. Accordingly, with an army in excess of 60,000 men engaged upon the siege of Numantia,[101] the building of seven garrison bases (ranging in size from 4ha–14.6ha),[102] distributed fairly evenly around the circuit, appears a reasonable decision. Indeed, because these camps were built astride the circumvallation, a significant economy of force could be achieved by making the enemy-facing part of the camp perimeter the effective front line. This is in marked contrast to the situation at Masada, where the two main garrison camps (B, 1.99ha and F, 1.96ha)[103] were recessed behind the line and played no direct role in its defence (*34, 35* and *colour plate 14*). However, the topographically-determined encirclement of this fortress with distinct western and eastern sectors each containing one of these bases, highlights the importance of an appropriate allocation of force. With rapid reinforcement from the other sector an unlikely prospect, Flavius Silva's decision to set up two garrison bases acting independently as the operational headquarters and strategic reserve for their respective halves of the circuit, was entirely sensible. No doubt the same rationale informed the establishment of two camps, one on either side of the target at Agrigentum (262 BC), Corfinium and (initially) at Numantia.[104]

35 Camps B and C at Masada with the Wadi Sebbe in between

Although the system that operated at Bethar (AD 135) is far from clear, two large camps have been located on the high ground to the south of the site.[105] Camp A, at 8.3ha, was significantly larger than camp B (2.6ha), but their proximity (B being built c.200m to the east of A) requires some explanation, particularly as there are no other confirmed camp sites along the known circuit (17). The answer here probably lies in the fact that the only effective approach to the town was along the saddle to the north of these two positions making this the crucial sector in which to achieve a concentration of force. Thus, whilst the garrison of camp A prepared to undertake direct approaches[106] or to resist any major sortie, that of camp B may have had the less glamorous task of maintaining patrols along the circumvallation. The section of the line lying to the north of the Rephaim Valley might also have been furnished with a separate sector garrison, and this may well have been housed within the camp that Schulten located[107] on the eastern spur, north of the stream. However, an examination of the ground by the author failed to find any trace of this feature, and the nature of the terrain would, in any event, seem to have precluded the siting of any major encampment in this area.

(ii) Smaller camps and 'blockhouses'

In circumstances where the blockade was maintained from a single large garrison base or where there was more than one such encampment and the circuit was either lengthy or crossed dissected terrain, then operational efficiency would have required the provision of supplementary interval forts. Such fortifications could play a direct role in line defence (providing fire-support and local reserves for immediate counter-attacks) not to mention accommodating the guard set over the works and acting as subordinate command and control centres. Depending upon the siege in question, these secondary camps could vary dramatically in size, a matter that would have had a direct bearing upon the tasks that they were capable of performing. Both Masada and Machaerus present an interesting diversity of these smaller camps.

At Masada, there are two camps of the same 'intermediate' size of 0.43ha,[108] which may be distinguished from the other, smaller posts, by their performance of specialist functions. As camp C was set back behind the gate tower on the eastern circumvallation, it is reasonable to assume that it would have been the base for patrolling the dead ground in advance of the wall between the Wadis Sebbe and Nimre, for which task its cavalry garrison[109] would have been most suitable. Meanwhile, two of the gateways of camp E open through the line of circumvallation, suggesting that in the event of a serious sally, it would have been a suitable point of retreat for the crews working on the assault ramp (its multiple gateways reducing the dangers of bunching). Equally, its proximity to both the ramp and to the 'engineering yard' suggests that its garrison may have been charged with the point defence of these two sites.

The remaining posts at Masada[110] would not have required such a significant establishment. Camps A and D (both 0.24ha) would have served as police posts for their assigned proportion of the wall line but might also have assisted with logistical duties in providing escorts for the supply convoys arriving along the Dead Sea and En-Gedi roads respectively. Camp G (0.19ha) would have carried out a similar police function in respect of the south-western area. Its unusual shape may have resulted from a re-modelling that saw the insertion of a heavy artillery platform to allow for a more effective domination of the Nahal Masada (36). Camp H (0.15ha), isolated on the southern plateau edge, would have proved a useful observation point enjoying oversight of enemy activity on the mesa-top. It has also been suggested[111] that the middle turret on the eastern wall (turret 8) may have had an attached annexe which could have acted as a 'guard chamber'. Given its location roughly 500m from both camps C and D, such a facility would have assisted with the proper manning of the turrets. If this was the case, then turret 8 might be thought of as a 'blockhouse' in the sense of a small, defended post in an isolated position (37).

As the main 'legionary' camp at Machaerus has not been located, there would appear to be very limited accommodation available for the besieging force. If the reality of all the camps suggested for the site can be accepted, then there are 17 different posts distributed around the circuit, ranging in size between 0.02ha–0.19ha.[112] However, the way in which the fort(let)s around the circumvallation varied in size was not the result of arbitrary factors . Essentially, it would seem that the corner angles of the roughly quadrangular system were covered by the larger establishments (although at 0.19ha, camp B, the largest of all, would not have been much bigger than the smallest camp on the Masada circuit).[113] The intervening ground was then protected by distinctly smaller posts (at 0.02ha,[114] 'camp' C can fairly be termed a blockhouse). Presumably this system envisaged the apportionment of responsibility for each 'quarter' of the investment between the anchor-point forts, with the interval *castella* being manned on a rotating basis by guard details despatched from each. As we have already seen, an important function of some of these smaller posts was to act as firing positions for heavy artillery. Camp H (at 0.18ha, the second largest of the forts)[115] would seem to contradict this model, but a 'full-sized' camp in a median position on the western front would have been necessary to block the ridge on which it stands (*colour plate 15*) and to provide reinforcement if the troops occupying camp Q were threatened by a serious enemy sortie.

36 Camp G at Masada

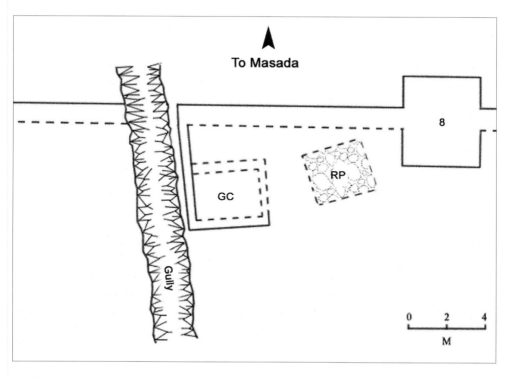

37 The 'blockhouse' at turret 8 on the circumvallation at Masada with guard chamber (GC) and rubble platform for possible artillery stand (RP)

The contrast between the multiplicity of small fortifications at Machaerus and the fewer, larger camps on the longer circumvallation at Masada (despite the Tenth legion being responsible for both) can be attributed to the greater danger of a sally in force by the more numerous defenders of the former site. The Masada scenario involved far less risk of a concerted enemy attack, and a looser supervisory regime based upon wall patrols rather than the occupation of fixed positions may have been deemed sufficient provision.

(c) Length of circuit and other metrical considerations

Tactical decisions as to the siting of any line of circumvallation would have been dependent upon such matters as the relative strength of the parties, the nature of the terrain and the overall strategic objective that the encirclement was intended to fulfil. The importance of achieving a correct balance between these various factors is thrown into stark relief by the Caesarian experience at Dyrrachium.

Although Caesar's own account of this episode represents a brave attempt at self-justification,[116] it is apparent that whatever the strategic merit behind the decision to pin Pompey's superior force against the coast, the tactical execution of the plan can be severely criticized. As soon as the two sides began their war of position in the coastal hills (*colour plate 1*), it should have been clear that Caesar's considerable disadvantage in manpower terms would quickly be translated into potential weakness on the battlefield. Pompey's prompt reaction in contesting control of the hill-tops and in forcing the extension of the Caesarian line to cover a distance of nearly 16 miles, severely stretched his opponent's resources. The subsequent measures taken to shore up the vulnerable southern sector (adding over a mile of entrenchments to the existing works)[117] meant that the besiegers were spread too thinly to prevent a Pompeian offensive from breaching the line. Only a savage counter-attack restored the situation. That his army had narrowly escaped envelopment could not have escaped Caesar's notice, but his stubbornness in maintaining his positions regardless, invited disaster. It was only after a second reverse on the same front (which a younger Pompey would surely have exploited more fully) that Caesar ordered a strategic withdrawal in a tacit acknowledgement of the failure of his scheme.

(i) The length of the line(s)

It is apparent from this example that Caesar had committed himself to an investment without sufficient regard to either the balance of opposing forces or to the calibre of the opposition and it was luck rather than better judgement that saved him from complete defeat. In this case, the equation of manpower with length of circuit (22,000 men[118] on an eventual 17-mile front) was heavily weighted against the besieger (particularly when the defenders enjoyed a numerical superiority of *c*.3:1) and only the most self-confident commander would ever have contemplated mounting a siege under such circumstances.

Extensive lines of circumvallation were, however, by no means rare in the Roman experience, even if some reports as to length must be regarded as grossly exaggerated or mistakenly transcribed (Appian's 1,200 stades/*c*.219km for the Caesarian circuit at Dyrrachium or Plutarch's 300 stades/*c*.55km for Crassus' blockade of Spartacus (71 BC) near Thurii).[119] For example, ambitious but credible systems include those built

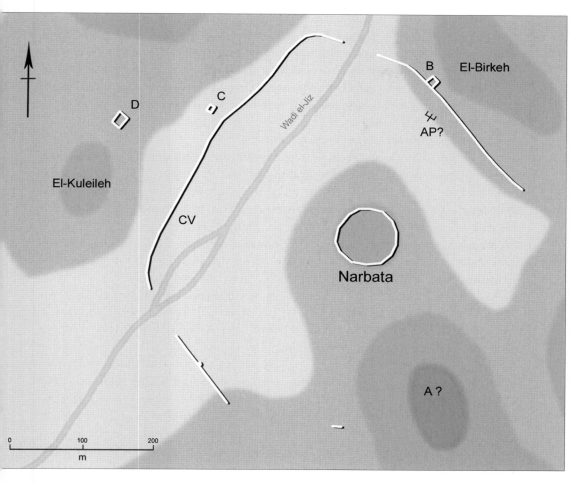

El-Birkeh

B

AP?

D

C

El-Kuleileh

CV

Wadi el-Jiz

Narbata

A ?

0   100   200
        m

38 The siege system at Narbata with camps (A to D), possible artillery position (AP) and circumvallation (CV)

by Scipio at Numantia (48 stades/c.8.8km),[120] by Octavian at Perusia (56 stades/c.10.2 km),[121] by Titus at Jerusalem (39 stades/c.7.1km)[122] and, above all, by Caesar at Alesia (where the combined course of the circum/contravallation amounted to c.35.7km).[123] In all of these examples, the common denominator appears to have been a sufficiency of force allowing the demands of large-scale construction and of subsequent manning to be absorbed without compromising the combat capability of the besieging army. For operations involving fewer troops, a contraction of the overall perimeter might be expected in line with the reduction in manpower (although Dyrrachium demonstrates this need not always have been the case!). Thus at Machaerus and Masada, where only one legion and an unspecified number of auxiliaries were committed, the circumference of the works amounted to c.3.5km and c.4.5km respectively. At the latter site, the fact that much of the circuit would have been virtually unassailable did not deter the Romans from constructing their wall to the same gauge and standard throughout. Beyond any symbolic dimension, this determination to complete a continuous line makes it even less likely that sectors would have been left 'open' at other sites.[124] The shortest circumvallation that we have evidence for is that at Narbata (*38*), where the recovered line extends over a distance of 1.5km,[125] although a further 800m should probably be added to this total to cover the missing stretch to the south and south-east of the town. In fact, it would be very difficult to envisage a full circumvallation having much less of a perimeter if only for reasons of simple geometry.

In order to determine the theoretical minimum circumference of a line of circumvallation, the following assumptions will be made:

(a) that the target has a (modest) diameter of 100m

(b) That an equidistant line could be drawn around the target at the optimal range of 300m (see below).

Applying the formula of $2\pi R$ to obtain the circumference would then result in the following calculation:

2 x 350 m (the radius) x 3.142 = 2,199.40 m.

Although this calculation is subject to the operation of several variables (such as the size of the target, the nature of the terrain and whether the defenders had access to artillery), it does provide a useful yardstick as to the minimum requirement for the extension of a fully encircling line. Of course, topographical considerations might have sometimes meant that an enemy centre could be isolated by less extensive works (particularly promontory sites such as Cremna).

(ii) The range of the line from the target

An important consideration in the siting of a line of circumvallation would have been the distance at which it was to have been set from the enemy-held positions. This decision would have been determined both by topographical factors and the character of the siege in question. If a passive blockade was intended, then the circuit could be placed at some remove from the target as it would not be required to support offensive approaches. However, the formula outlined above makes it clear that the further the circumvallation was situated from the target, the longer its circumference would be, thus increasing the burden of supervision. On the other hand, where more aggressive tactics were to be employed, it would be important to maximize the contribution of a well-sited line both in providing effective artillery support and in furnishing a secure point of retreat for working parties exposed to hostile sallies.

The earliest passive blockade for which we have specific information as to the range between the investment and the enemy wall is that of Capua, where the interval was stated to have been a distance of 2 stades.[126] Beyond the fact that several engagements were fought with the Campanian cavalry on the open ground before the contravallation, the issue here was to be decided by time rather than by assault[127] and, as we have already seen, the design of the line reflected this essentially defensive stance. Accordingly, the decision to set the contravallation at a range of c.360m from the city enceinte may have been a deliberate attempt to provide the closest possible investment whilst minimizing the impact of enemy artillery fire from the numerous machines mounted on their walls. Whilst the Roman encirclement may have been within the technical range of (some) such pieces, any resulting fire directed at the works would probably have been too inaccurate and of insufficient kinetic impact to have been worth maintaining.

Another occasion upon which the circumvallation was built 'a considerable distance' from the target was during the siege of Praeneste (82 BC) by Sulla's lieutenant Ofella.[128] Although the precise interval is not reported, there must have been a wide gap between the city walls and the encirclement as the Younger Marius was able to march out and fortify a position within this 'no-man's land'. However, as Sulla's objective was to use the siege as a device to entice relief efforts by other Marian forces (which could then be defeated in turn by his field army) and because famine and not fighting was to be the tool of reduction, it was appropriate for Ofella's men to take up position at some remove from the walls of Praeneste.

At Numantia, another overtly passive blockade, the circumvallation was laid out so as to derive the maximum benefit from the terrain, and the town walls on the hill-top were only within artillery range from the river-front rampart of the fort at Alto Real. Although it is likely that the defenders were not confined within the town enceinte but were spread more widely over the hillslope and adjacent foothills, probably protected by extemporized field works, these advanced positions would only have been open to bombardment from a very limited proportion of the circuit. In fact, although at its closest (by Alto Real), the circumvallation may have approached to within 200m of these putative advanced positions, on average it would seem to have maintained itself at an interval of c.600m-700m, with significant sectors being located over a kilometre away. Not only was this alignment of the rampart a product of careful topographical selection but the wide *intervallum* would also have given the besiegers an opportunity to order up reserves when any hostile sortie was seen to develop.

In cases where the circumvallation was employed more aggressively as the base-line for other, direct approaches, then different tactical priorities would have determined the question of siting. An important function of the circumvallation in these circumstances would have been to provide firing positions for the artillery covering the crews working on the assault preparations. This is best illustrated at Cremna, where stone mounds on the line of the contravallation between turrets 5 and 6 (c.150m-175m from the city wall) have been identified as reinforced bases for artillery to provide suppressive fire for work details raising the siege mound.[129] The subsequent masking of these positions by the bulk of the mound demonstrates that their construction was only ever intended as a temporary expedient, with redundancy an inevitable consequence of their success. Somewhat similarly, at Machaerus, it is no coincidence that where the circumvallation approaches to within 200m of the foot of the citadel on its western front (where the

39 Circumvallation at Machaerus descending the southern Wadi el-Misneqa with camps F and G denoted

assault ramp was under construction), the wall attains its maximum thickness of 2.4m. This may have been insufficient for mounting catapults, but it would certainly have been adequate for allowing archers to be posted along the parapet. However, flanking fire from light artillery could have been delivered from the blockhouse (*39*) of camp G (*c.*270m from the enemy wall) whilst a heavier bombardment could have been delivered from camp Q (*c.*210m from the fortress enceinte).

The possibility of artillery carrying out a more directly offensive role, by inflicting actual structural damage to the enemy defences, has already been suggested for the platforms that were built in advance of turret 4 at Cremna where the contravallation projects out in a bastion-like trace (to within 125m of the city wall) to accommodate these positions.

A further advantage of a relatively closely-set line, is that it would have allowed assault units to form up in safety within striking distance of the enemy and would have provided a secure place of retreat both for repulsed storming parties and for construction crews overwhelmed by a sortie. At Masada, the circumvallation at the foot of the Λευκη, approaches to within 280m of the fortress, and although the enemy walls may have been within technical range of any artillery placed here (albeit that the firing trajectory would probably have proved unfeasible), its real significance lies in its utility for the assault preparations. Not only would a close-in line have provided security (the multiple gates through the wall at camp E are significant pointers in this regard as well), but it also allowed the engineering yard to be sited less than 200m from the foot of the assault ramp.

This would have been an important consideration as the fabrication of the iron–clad siege tower and the 'great ram' would have been undertaken here within the shelter of a walled compound set behind the circumvallation. Transporting such bulky equipment over any significant distance would otherwise have been an unwelcome prospect.

(iii) Labour and time

Many variables would have affected the time taken to construct a line of investment (troop availability and experience; type of circumvallation required; material availability and terrain; scale of any hostile interdiction) and the simple comparison of individual siege campaigns is not very helpful. Furthermore, although it may be suggested that a stone wall would have involved greater effort to construct than a dump rampart or that experienced men would have taken less time to raise field works than novices, such observations cannot be sustained from the evidence at our disposal. The *a priori* calculations made by Roth[130] and Richmond[131] that the circumvallation at Masada took either five days (the former) or a week (the latter) to complete, may be substantially correct, but we have no means of evaluating the accuracy of such statements short of undertaking experimental reconstruction on a repetitive basis to determine whether familiarity with the necessary techniques had a significant bearing upon performance.

Given these limitations, it is unwise to do more than note what little the sources tell us about the time taken to construct such works. At Sparta (195 BC),[132] the 50,000 men at Flamininus' disposal built 'siege works' to seal the open spaces around the city to prevent any escape (presumably this involved raising a line of circumvallation) and completed the task within three days. However, only a proportion of the Roman army could have been engaged in actual construction at any one time, as significant numbers must have been posted as a covering force (particularly in view of the success of an earlier sortie mounted by Nabis) whilst other formations were deployed to mount harrying attacks against the defenders. When Caesar's veterans (eight legions and an uncertain number of auxiliaries) appeared before Vellaunodunum (52 BC),[133] they succeeded in surrounding the *oppidum* with a circumvallation within two days, prompting the defenders to surrender out of despair. Titus, with four legions and large contingents of allied troops, threw a wall 39 stades/*c*.7.1km long with 13 redoubts attached, around Jerusalem in three days, although Josephus does point out that this work was completed in rapid order because of the intense rivalry engendered between units.[134] This competitive spirit was deliberately fostered by Titus and ensured that this extensive system was operational in a remarkably short time.[135] However, the comparative value of the Jerusalem example should not be overstated because of these exceptional circumstances, and to use it as a general measure of Roman field practice (as did Richmond for his calculation above of the time taken by the Tenth legion to extend the circumvallation around Masada) would be misleading.

The role of circumvallation in ensuring the thorough isolation of the target would have made this the most effective means of enforcing a blockade for a besieger with ample manpower reserves. It also proved a useful preparation for the commencement of more direct methods of reduction and it is the evidence for the structures associated with these forward offensive strategies that will now be discussed.

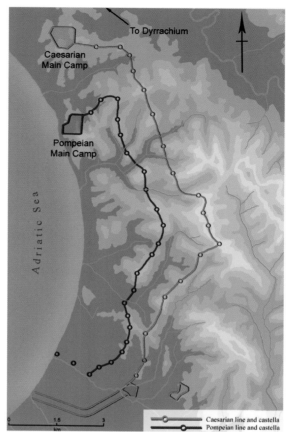

Right: 1 The siege system at Dyrrachium. *After Veith 1920*

Below: 2 The siege system at Alesia

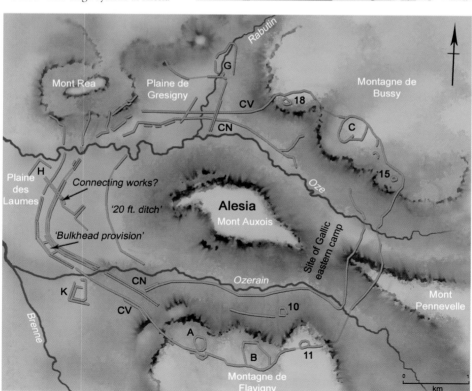

Left: 3 Artillery positions in advance of Turret 4 at Cremna

Below: 4 The siege system at Numantia

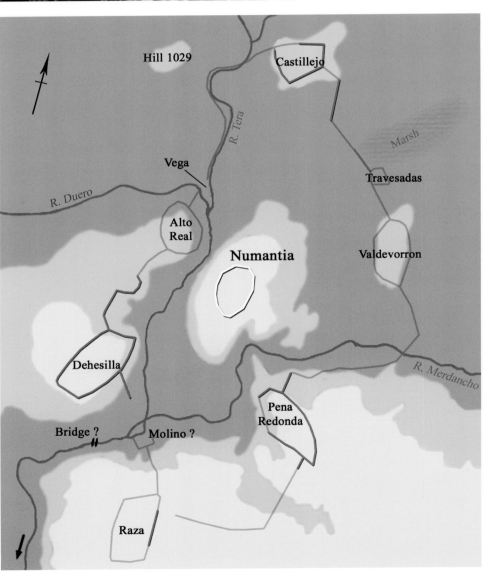

Hill 1029

Castillejo

R. Tera

Marsh

Vega

Travesadas

R. Duero

Alto Real

Numantia

Valdevorron

Dehesilla

R. Merdancho

Pena Redonda

Bridge ?

Molino ?

Raza

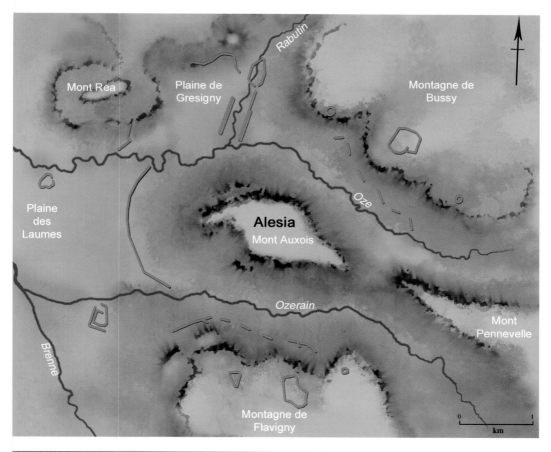

Mont Rea

Plaine de
Gresigny

Rabutin

Montagne de
Bussy

Plaine
des
Laumes

Oze

Alesia
Mont Auxois

Ozerain

Mont
Pennevelle

Brenne

Montagne de
Flavigny

0   1
km

Above: 5 First phase screening works at
Alesia. *After Benard 1987*

Left: 6 Alexandrium from the east

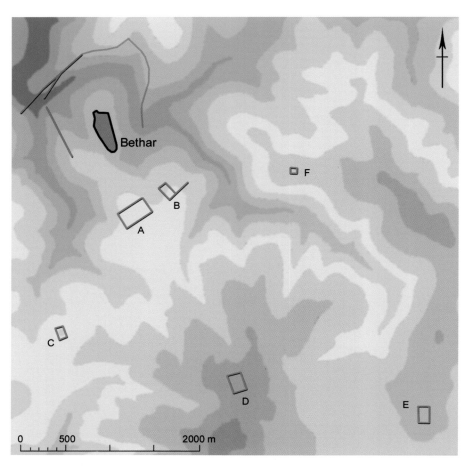

Bethar

A

B

C

D

E

F

0   500   2000 m

Left: 7 The siege system at Bethar showing the detached camp trace. *After Kennedy & Riley 1990*

Below: 8 Bethar from the north

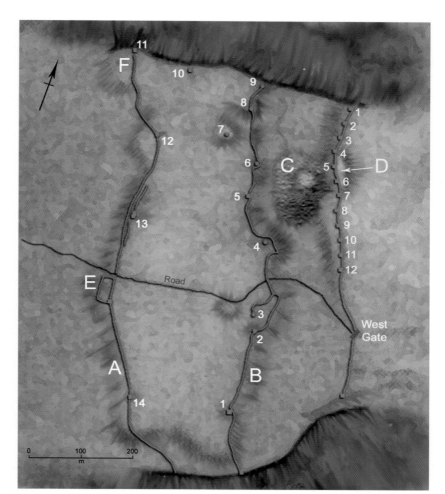

Right: 9 The siege system at Cremna (*after Mitchell et al 1995*) with circumvallation (A) contravallation (B) siege mound (C) counter–mound (D) 'HQ compound' (E) *cannabae* (F)

Below: 10 Narbata from the south

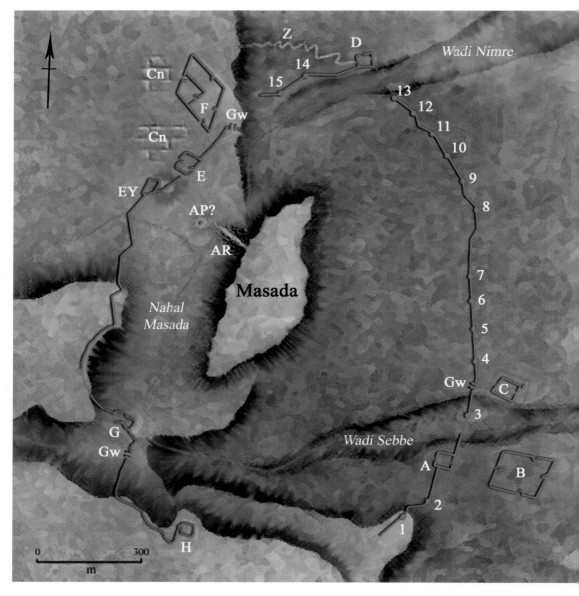

11 The siege system at Masada with Roman camps (A to H), possible artillery position (AP), assault ramp (AR), *cannabae* (Cn), engineering yard (EY), gateways through the circumvallation (Gw) and 'zig-zag' path (Z)

Opposite above: 12 The siege system at Machaerus (*after Strobel 1974a and Kennedy and Riley 1990*) with Roman camps and possible camps (A to Q), aqueduct (aq), assault ramp (AR), possible *baulager* (bl), cleared platform (cp), circumvallation (cv) and gateway (gw)

Opposite below: 13 The circumvallation south-west of Machaerus with camp E (artillery platforms arrowed)

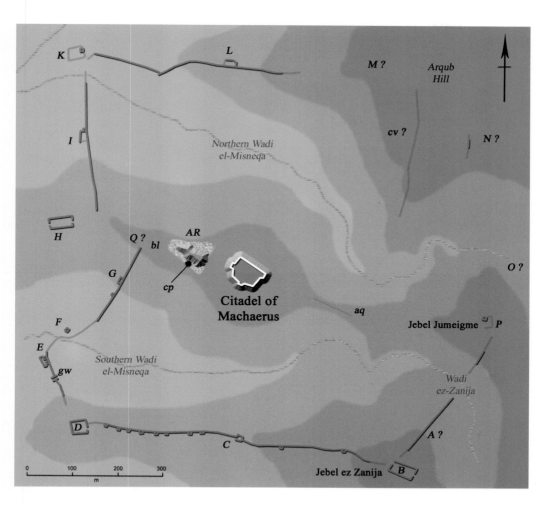

Above: 14 Camp F at Masada with the assault ramp behind

Left: 15 Camp H blocking the western ridge at Machaerus

Below left: 16 The assault ramp at Machaerus with camp H behind

Below right: 17 Probable site of Scipio's river crossing at Numantia

6

ASSAULT RAMPS AND SIEGE MOUNDS

Even though the classical sources do not draw any terminological distinction between the assault ramp and the siege mound, the different tactical functions performed by these two structures should encourage us to adopt a stricter semantic approach. In order to be clear, the term 'assault ramp' will be used here to mean any structure raised to parallel the height of a defensive work (or, at least, to reach its base), enabling the passage of storming parties and/or the mounting of engines capable of effecting a breach. On the other hand, a 'siege mound' should be understood as a structure raised to parallel or overtop the defences allowing oversight of the defenders and the advantageous emplacement of artillery. Thus an assault ramp can be recognized as a direct agent of reduction (by enabling the assault to be pressed home), whereas a siege mound should be viewed as a supporting tool, facilitating the delivery of the assault in its immediate vicinity.

THE ROMAN USE OF ASSAULT RAMPS AND SIEGE MOUNDS

Assault ramps were the first real siege works, being built to counter the increasing strength, height and defensive depth of urban enceintes. Their initial appearance in Hittite contexts[1] was followed by their employment as a standard element of the Assyrian and Persian siege repertoire,[2] but although the knowledge of this technique would presumably have been transferred to the Greeks, assault ramps were a comparatively rare phenomenon in *polis* warfare before the Hellenistic period.[3] This apparent reticence may perhaps be ascribed to the scale of the required undertaking: most city-states had inadequate manpower to allow the completion of such structures whilst simultaneously maintaining a sufficiently strong field army to deter any sortie in force from the defenders. This rationale may also explain why the adoption of the assault ramp was similarly delayed in the Roman world (their reported occurrence at Fidenae (494 BC),[4] Veii (403 BC)[5] and Satricum (386 BC),[6] can probably be attributed to anachronism). Meanwhile, we should not expect the early introduction of the siege mound given that its effectiveness relied almost entirely upon the availability of artillery, and it is highly unlikely that the Romans would have had access to the necessary engine technology until well into the fourth century BC.

The first concerted programme of raising these structures did not take place until the First Punic War. The large armies that were then at the disposal of Roman commanders (sometimes exceeding 100,000 in strength), allowed the construction of ambitious siege works which, at Panormus (254 BC), Lipara (252 BC) and Lilybaeum (250-249 BC) included the raising of assault ramps.[7] These were fairly simple structures designed to allow rams access to the enemy walls by bridging approach obstacles such as moats and ditches, but their contribution would appear to have been decisive in bringing about the collapse of parts of the enceinte at both Panormus and Lilybaeum. Perhaps the earliest reference to a siege mound in a Roman context can be inferred from Corvus' siege of Cales (335 BC?)[8] where a mound was built and penthouses and towers advanced. Given the consul's express concern to avoid casualties, this structure could have been a siege mound in support of the engineers attempting to sap the enemy wall rather than a ramp, which would have entailed a risky (and costly) assault. If we believe Silius Italicus claims that an *agger* was raised at Capua,[9] then such a structure, too, would have been a siege mound as no assault was contemplated here.

Following their successful employment against the Carthaginians, assault ramps quickly became a conventional tool for those Roman commanders who favoured direct methods of approach over the blockade. Indeed, the employment of assault ramps can be seen as part of the wider technical competence that slowly disseminated throughout the Roman army, so that the raising of these structures became one of the standard field works that soldier-engineers might be expected to undertake. This is not to say that ramps were built to a universally high standard: at Atrax (198 BC), although rams succeeded in demolishing a section of the defenders' wall, a mobile tower (brought up to clear the breach of Macedonians) was caught in a wheel rut in the loose soil of the poorly compacted ramp and rendered useless.[10] Other engineers experienced difficulties when the defenders sought to undermine their *aggeres*, although counter-tunnels (as at the Piraeus, 87-86 BC)[11] or the simple expedient of dumping more soil than the enemy could hope to remove (as may have been Crassus' response before the stronghold of the Sotiates, 56 BC)[12] might have counteracted such initiatives. As the most pressing threat (at least to ramps with a significant timber component) was that of an incendiary attack in the course of a hostile sortie, the forward stationing of troops (as at Avaricum, 52 BC)[13] both to cover the work crews and to extinguish any fire that was ignited, was a sensible precaution if the laborious process of construction was not to be wasted.

Another consequence of an increasing familiarity with the requisite building techniques, was that assault ramps became increasingly ambitious in the scope of their function and form. What had once been intended as simple bridging tools to cross artificial obstacles before the enemy wall, were now expanded to overcome natural barriers as well. Thus Pompey threw several ramps across the deep ravine that fronted the western front of the Temple Mount at Jerusalem (63 BC),[14] whilst Censorinus completed an approach path for two enormous rams by filling in the lagoon beside the isthmus at Carthage (149 BC).[15] Whereas the example of Atrax shows how rams and mobile towers might have been deployed consecutively on the same ramp, the delay inherent in removing one engine and replacing it with another might have given the defenders time to re-group and re-fortify. Accordingly, as part of the general improvement in ramp construction, better provision was made for the simultaneous use of various engines at the *point d'appui*. This meant either widening and strengthening the ramp to allow multiple engine deployment, or fabricating large siege towers that could act as artillery station, assault bridge and ram housing combined. Not only would the resulting ramps have to be sufficiently robust to bear the burden stemming from these developed tactical roles, but care would also have to be taken over their gradient to enable the necessary superstructures to be raised into position. Such advanced ramps, characterized here as 'Avaricum-style' structures after the impressive example deployed by Caesar before the Gallic *oppidum*, had their origin in the first century BC and continued in use up until the Flavian suppression of the Jewish Revolt. Thereafter, despite the general swing in favour of strategies of assault over those of blockade, the use of assault ramps would appear to tail off dramatically, reflecting a general pattern whereby elaborate and technically-informed approaches were abandoned by the Roman army. Indeed, a rare, late appearance for the assault ramp at Pirisabora (AD 363),[16] where the ditches of the fortress were filled in to allow rams to be deployed, demonstrates a reversion to the earliest use of these structures as simple bridging tools.

Although the role of siege mounds was substantially usurped during the heyday of the combined function Avaricum-style ramp, the benefit of providing elevated artillery platforms ensured their continued employment in specialized circumstances. By way of illustration, although Caesar made no attempt to approach the walls of Uxellodunum (51 BC), he did raise a mound in order to interdict enemy access to an extra-mural spring.[17] However, despite the ascendancy of the assault ramp as the reductive tool of choice, much effort might still be expended upon the construction of single function siege mounds as in the two huge structures raised by Trebonius at Massilia (49 BC).[18] That the eclipse noted in the use of the assault ramp was not repeated in the case of the siege mound, can probably be attributed to the continuing need to provide close-fire support for storming parties and for sappers. This survival of siege mounds (e.g. at Cremna, AD 277-278 or at Bezabde, AD 360)[19] may be explicable in the context of the simpler techniques required to build these structures compared to the Avaricum-style ramps. After all, a simple artillery platform would only have needed sufficient bracing to bear the weight (and absorb the recoil) of the catapults emplaced upon it, whilst the assault ramp would also have had to withstand the considerably greater shock of each ram blow, not to mention the weight of many more men required to operate the additional engines.

FORM AND STRUCTURE

Whereas the archaeological examination of the siege works elements discussed so far might only require conventional small area excavation, such methods will prove inadequate for the investigation of ramps and mounds. These structures require the expenditure of considerable resources if they are to be examined systematically and only a limited number of such sites have received this attention. Apart from limited interventions on the ramp at Masada, Roman *aggeres* have remained unexcavated and for any archaeological perspective upon the way in which these structures were constructed, we must refer to roughly comparable structures built in the deeper past.[20]

But before discussing questions of form and construction, we should summarize those functional attributes of both ramps and mounds that responsible engineers would have needed to bear in mind.

As assault ramps were intended to play a direct role in effecting the fall of the defended centre, they had to be brought within striking distance of the enemy wall. If the reduction was to proceed by battery, then the ram(s) would have to be brought into contact with the target, although sufficient space had to be left at the foot of the wall to prevent any dislodged masonry from collapsing directly on top of the breaching engine.[21] Usually, therefore, the ramp needed to be sufficiently elevated to allow the ram(s) access to the enemy wall-base, although in circumstances where there was a pronounced batter, or where the object was to engage the parapet-top directly (as in the famous Assyrian reliefs depicting Lachish, *40*),[22] then the structure would have to be raised still further. The careful calculation of the necessary height was also important in those cases where the ramp was meant to allow storming parties access to the defenders' wall-top, either via gangways extended from the structure itself or from siege towers emplaced upon it. Another significant factor was the gradient of the ramp, as a sensible (and constant) angle of inclination would have to be maintained over the long axis of the structure in order to winch/drag/push engines, towers and other pre-fabricated housings into position at the strike face. Also, the summit area itself would have to provide a sufficient, flattened area for the accommodation of the machinery etc. Given the importance of achieving a *schwerpunkt* (a sufficient concentration of force) at the point of attack and the necessity of rapidly reinforcing an initial breakthrough, the ramp would ideally provide an adequate forming-up zone for the storming party and an avenue of advance for the support troops. Although these various requirements might be modified to reflect the prevailing circumstances, the key specification must have been that the ramp was sufficiently robust to carry out its designated task(s).

For siege mounds, the overriding objective was to provide supporting fire for direct approaches in their immediate vicinity, so the structures had to be placed in sufficient proximity to the enemy enceinte to suppress activity along the parapet and to silence any hostile artillery. If the performance of this task demanded the raising of a supplementary siege tower on the summit (perhaps to confront secondary turrets added to the enemy wall or a formal counter-mound), then the siege mound had to be sturdy enough to support such a superstructure. Presumably the number of batteries that were to be operated from it would have determined the actual dimensions of the firing platform on the mound-top.

(a) Initial site selection and ground clearance

Although the tactical task assigned to the structure would have determined issues such as the distance it was to be sited from the enemy wall (e.g., an assault ramp planned with an elevated target in mind needed to be started at some considerable distance from the wall if it was to maintain a suitable gradient for moving siege paraphernalia along its

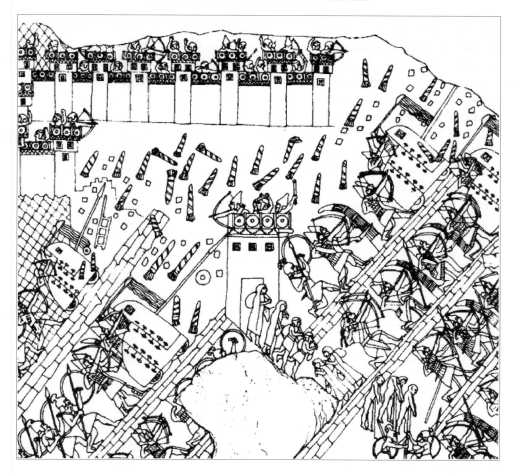

40 Segment III of the Lachish Relief showing Assyrian assault ramps in action

course), basic topographical and other physical considerations would also have exerted a significant influence. At Masada, when deciding upon the location of his ramp, Silva had little option but to take advantage of the natural stepping stone provided by the hard chalk spur of the Λευκη (*2* and *colour plate 14*) which considerably reduced the vertical interval between the mesa-top and the surrounding terrain. Similarly, at Cremna, when Terentius Marcianus took the decision to establish artillery superiority over the defenders by building a siege mound, the most logical place to raise such a structure was at the narrowest point of the valley flanking the western defences of the city.

Pre-existing extra-mural structures may also have exerted some influence on site selection, particularly if they offered labour crews cover in the initial stages of construction. The recycling of such buildings through demolition also formed a potentially significant source of raw materials for the *agger*-builder, as the evidence of the Persian ramp at Palaepaphos (which incorporated architectural fragments from a nearby shrine)[23] readily indicates. In a Roman context, we are informed that the destruction of the suburbs of

41 The cleared platform south of the assault ramp at Machaerus

Heraclea (191 BC) provided M'. Acilius Glabrio with sufficient material to advance three separate ramps,[24] whilst the large ramp thrown across the isthmus at Laodicea (43 BC) was 'composed of stones and all sorts of material brought from the suburban houses and tombs'.[25] Similarly, at the Piraeus (87 BC), Sulla ordered that the Long Walls be pulled down in order that the stone, timber and earth that comprised the same could be reused in the huge ramp that he raised against the walls of the port.[26] The usefulness of such *spolia* was often recognized by the defenders, and the self-demolition of their own suburbs by the Xanthians (42 BC) was a deliberate act to deny this harvest to Brutus' men.[27]

This demolition of extra-mural buildings not only furnished raw materials, but it may also have been necessary to clear a path along which the ramp/mound could be advanced. Even where buildings may not have been present, an initial process of ground clearance and/or levelling would have preceded any formal construction. At Lachish, a layer of ash and the charred remains of olive and terebinth recovered from the base of the Assyrian ramp suggests that the undergrowth abutting the tel-slope had been fired as a preliminary to the building process.[28] In a similar vein, there is clear evidence for preparatory works at the site of the assault ramp at Machaerus, where a broad apron to the north, south and west of the ramp (*41*) would appear to have been deliberately scarped, the soil cover being stripped in places down to the bare bedrock. Not only would this process have provided a level platform, cleared of any obstruction for the raising of the ramp, but it would also have allowed the collection of much of the eventual fill for the structure. Although the widespread 'quarried areas' reported at Cremna,[29] are not located at the precise site of the siege mound, their occurrence in the *intervallum* zone both to the west and north west of the structure, implies that the extensive programme of soil-stripping carried out in the vicinity can be correlated with the progress of mound construction. Literary confirmation for this process of ground clearance can be obtained from the description of how Trebonius' earthworks at Massilia were advanced, the pioneers working on the siege mound being preceded by a *testudo* (or mobile penthouse), which covered the troops engaged upon levelling the valley floor in preparation for the forward extension of the embankment.[30]

(b) Scale and time

Although the construction of a line of circumvallation involved the dedication of considerable labour resources, the resulting scheme conveyed little of the same sense of imminent threat that the sheer bulk of an advancing *agger* achieved. Indeed, the simple size of the ramps and mounds remains the single most striking feature of those ancient siege systems where they survive, their mass all the more impressive in the knowledge that they were raised in the face of the enemy, with the pioneers being exposed to missile fire and the threat of hostile sorties.

There are relatively few accounts which provide us with details as to the dimensions of these structures or of the time taken to raise them and it is usually only those examples that were considered particularly noteworthy by their contemporaries for which we have any information (making the extrapolation of general conclusions somewhat problematic).

For example, Caesar reports[31] that his complex structure before the walls of Avaricum was 330ft broad and 80ft high and took 25 days for his men to complete, figures that presumably were intended to impress the reader with both the scale of the endeavour and the industry of his army. We are left with the impression that his earlier ramps at Noviodunum and at the stronghold of the Aduatuci (both 57 BC), were completed within a far shorter time-span, even though each ramp had to be sufficiently robust to accommodate siege towers and that the terrain and the strength of the defences created difficulties at both sites.[32]

The Josephan account of the various ramps raised in the course of Titus' siege of Jerusalem (6) provides some interesting pointers as to methods of construction (see below), but remains vague as to the precise size of the structures in question. Certain general observations may, however, be possible. The three ramps thrown against the Third wall (the weakest part of the enemy enceinte), took considerably less time to build than the 15 days that it took to penetrate this barrier.[33] Indeed, from the narrative, it seems fair to deduce that the ramps must have been completed within a week if the subsequent delay inherent in deploying the rams, in battering the walls, in resisting various hostile sorties, in repairing the damage caused by the incendiary attacks, in fabricating the siege towers and moving them into position and, finally, in effecting the decisive breach, is to be accommodated. The 'double' ramps (see later) deployed against the First wall and the Antonia, clearly much more impressive structures, took 17 days to complete.[34] As one of these was piled up across the Struthion pool, it appears that Titus was more concerned with the precise point of attack rather than with any difficulty over his approach path. Following the destruction of these structures, their replacements (four still larger ramps raised against the Antonia alone) were completed within 21 days, notwithstanding the timber shortage that meant that tree-felling had to be carried out at a distance of 90 stades/*c.*16.5km from the city.[35]

The fall of the Antonia was followed by the demolition of the fortress for reuse within the next great ramp extended against the Temple portico which took seven days to build (the speed presumably reflecting the concentration of legionary labour on this one task and the ready availability of the necessary materials).[36] This structure would seem to have functioned as an approach path that allowed the Romans to deploy their forces directly against the outer court of the Temple (either via four separate *aggeres* or two 'pairs', presumably allocated one per legion as before). The final phase of earthwork construction involved the attack on the Upper City, which proceeded by means of legionary-built ramps thrown against the Herodian palace complex on the west and auxiliary-built structures crossing the ravine between the Temple Mount and the Upper City (an awkward task which demonstrates that construction skills were widely disseminated throughout Titus' army). All these works were completed within 18 days of 'hard labour', although the badly-shaken morale of the defenders probably meant that resistance had become far less effective.[37] In summary therefore, the various ramps advanced at Jerusalem took 7-21 days to complete depending upon the complexity of the task, the number of troops allocated and the availability of the necessary raw materials.

Following his initial reverse at the Third wall, Titus seems to have ensured that the subsequent structures raised by his troops were in the combined function Avaricum-style to avoid the delays caused by the need to bring up towers in support of the rams. These sophisticated ramps must have taken much longer to build than relatively simple bridging structures designed to cross obstacle fields in front of the enemy wall. However, there is little in our sources to confirm this supposition beyond noting that the ditches at Pirisabora were filled in by Julian's troops in the course of just one evening. Often, we can only speculate as to the time it would have taken to construct even those structures for which we have some dimensional information. Thus, although we are told that the ramp advanced across the isthmus at Laodicea by Cassius was 2 stades in length,[38] as we have no knowledge of the width of this structure or even, whether it was entirely land-bound, the question of the time that it took to construct must be left open, particularly as there is no means of assessing what (if any) delay would have been occasioned by Dolabella's fleet.

Fortunately, a limited number of assault ramps survive in sufficiently complete condition to allow us to reconstruct their original dimensions with some confidence. The first phase Assyrian ramp at Lachish has been calculated as having an overall length of *c.*60m, a basal width of *c.*75m reducing to *c.*25m at the *point d'appui* and a vertical elevation of *c.*15m.[39] The Persian ramp at Palaepaphos would seem to have been *c.*43m long, *c.*63m wide at its broadest but only a maximum of 3m in height over the berm in front of the town wall.[40] The 'unfinished' ramp at Machaerus was 85m long, *c.*15m wide at its tail and *c.*35m wide at the strike-face, with a maximum height of *c.*12m.[41] The surviving elements of the ramp at Masada show a structure 225m long with a basal width that varies between 50m-200m, and an artificial fill of *c.*25m-30m in height.[42] Finally, the Sassanian ramp at Dura-Europos was 40m long and extended to a maximum height of 12.5m.[43]

Even such a limited sample demonstrates the variety of size and shape that might be taken by different assault ramps as they attempted to overcome the topographical and artificial

42 The siege mound at Cremna with the town wall behind

challenges of individual sites, with such factors as the elevation of the defensive circuit and the width of the obstacle field exerting considerable influence upon the building process.

As far as siege mounds are concerned, we are faced with more acute problems of imprecise reporting both as to structural dimensions and the time taken over construction. Although there is considerable information to hand regarding the method by which the mounds were raised by Trebonius at Massilia (see below), the sole dimension that we are given for the same is that their height attained 80ft.[44] No independent archaeological evidence exists for these structures, but from his analysis of the terrain and the likely tactical deployments made by the Caesarians, Stoffel estimated that the 'principal platform of attack was started on the slope of the hill of St Charles at (a range of) 350m from the enceinte'.[45] If this calculation is correct, then the structure advanced across the flanking valley of St Martin would have represented one of the largest single earthworks ever raised by the Roman army. This is all the more striking when it is realized that the function of this enormous embankment was simply to support the wooden towers from which suppressive (and counter-battery) fire could be directed against the enemy walls. Apart from the Massiliote example, the only siege mound for which we have any dimensional reference is Caesar's artillery position at Uxellodunum, reported to be 60ft high and accommodating a tower that extended for another 10 storeys.[46] If nothing else, it is clear that the mound would have been a robustly-built structure to have supported such a superstructure (and its complement of engines and crew). To date, the only siege mound to have been identified in the field is that at Cremna. This impressive structure (42), astride the valley flanking the western defences of the city, extends for a distance of 120m on its east–west axis with a maximum basal width of 140m and is up to 25m high.[47] The threat posed by this work was not lost on the defenders as they attempted to reinforce the curtain immediately to its fore with their own counter-mound, both to bolster the wall against Roman bombardment and to limit the besiegers' overlook potential.

(c) Methods of construction and composition

Although there may have been considerable variation in the form taken by assault ramps and siege mounds, it is probably fair to claim that the manner in which these structures were raised either followed the stone and earth dump-built method or the more elaborate timber-framed approach. The precise mode of construction would have been influenced by such matters as the availability of raw materials (particularly wood), the role to be performed by the structure, the degree of urgency in pressing the attack, and the competence of the troops assigned to the responsible labour details. However, the often ambiguous statements made in the sources and the lack of much detailed archaeological examination, means that many of the suggestions made here must necessarily be conjectural in nature. Of course, this uncertainty has not prevented several authorities from advancing their own hypotheses both as to the appearance of these structures and the building techniques employed in their raising, and the different reconstructions suggested for the ramp at Avaricum[48] indicate how a sketchy account in the classical texts can be made to accommodate a range of modern interpretations.

(i) Dump-built structures

The most obvious (and easiest) way to raise a mound or ramp is to pile up earth in a continuous process. By starting at some remove from the intended target, accretional deposition will result in a linear, tapering effect as each load of fill is transported to the front of the mounting heap of spoil. The maintenance of a gentle incline from the tail to the dump-face will be generally self-regulating as the work crews seek to ease the burden of their task. Of course, a simple pile of earth will not achieve stasis unless it is given time to settle (something inherently improbable in a siege context), and in order for the assailant to be able to make use of the structure its stability would have to be assured. The most likely method of ensuring this consolidation would involve a work detail following in the wake of the soil dumping parties to compact the deposited horizon by ramming.

To reduce soil creep in the first instance, it might be advisable to lay a basal course of large stone blocks across the width of the *agger* to anchor the subsequent deposits. Including a significant proportion of stone rubble within the matrix of the fill should also act to improve structural cohesion, both by increasing the mass of the ramp/mound and by locking the looser elements at a higher level. Increased stability could also be achieved by providing some form of revetment (e.g. stone kerbing, timber shuttering, wicker screens) along the margins of the structure, although the care devoted to such measures of reinforcement might depend upon the degree of interference from hostile sallies and the availability of the necessary materials.

The failure of Flamininus' attack on Atrax (198 BC) is instructive. Here, the Romans extended a ramp of loosely compacted earth[49] and proceeded to open a narrow breach in the town wall. When the Macedonian defenders formed a phalanx to block this gap there was insufficient room to charge the formation and their flanks were covered by the remaining wall circuit. Accordingly, the assailants brought up a siege tower to clear the breach, but as it was being dragged into position the tower caught in a wheel rut (presumably left by the rams) and tilted over at such a severe angle that both it and the

43 The Assyrian assault ramp at Lachish

siege had to be abandoned. The rutted approach path at Atrax is a graphic demonstration of the consequences of failing to provide a properly compacted surface (or, alternatively, a properly laid timber track) for the advance of siege engines.

From the archaeological evidence, it is apparent that the Assyrians took great care to ensure the stability of their ramp at Lachish (*43*). This comprised a collection of large field stones with an earth fill capped by 1m-thick stone-and-mortar conglomerate.[50] This 'cap' was repeated as a second, 1m-thick layer at the summit of the first phase ramp,[51] where it would have furnished the level, strengthened platform for the war engines (and may have acted to absorb some of the kinetic shock resulting from repeated ram strikes). Interestingly, the second phase ramp, raised to top the counter-mound built as an emergency measure by the defenders, would appear to have been a simple stone-piled structure.[52] As this presents an uneven finish without any reinforcing mortared lens, it may simply have been designed as an assault path for the infantry without engine support.

The Lydian assault ramp thrown up against the north-west corner of the defensive circuit at Old Smyrna, was built up with materials obtained from the demolition of extra-mural suburbs.[53] The resulting mass comprised relatively loose debris stemming from the dumping of an amorphous rather than a homogenous fill, but the whole structure would appear to have been given solidity by the deposition of large, coherent chunks of mud-brick (former walling?) towards the base of the ramp. However, despite being opened to a depth of 13m, the section did not reach ground level and, accordingly, it is not certain that these deposits were intended as core reinforcement. Distinct stratigraphic levels sloping from north to south, presumably representing separate dumping horizons, nonetheless allow us to reconstruct the building process as one whereby the construction crews engaged in progressive fill-tipping from the north (i.e. as one would expect, the ramp was advanced towards the town wall from a distant point beyond the enceinte).

In terms of Roman assault ramps, our best example of a dump-built *agger* is the structure built on the western ridge at Machaerus (*colour plate 16*). This ramp is comprised of medium-sized, roughly-fashioned stone blocks packed with an earth fill (and although the latter appears to have been washed out of the more exposed eastern face, there has been no noticeable deterioration in overall structural cohesion). Also, from the evidence of the eastern terminal, it would appear that a basal course of larger stones was first dumped in position before being covered by the smaller stones and the earth packing. Over a distance of 85m, this ramp rises to a height of *c.*12m making for a gentle inclined plane along which the siege engines could be advanced without much difficulty. Whereas it has been suggested[54] that the Tenth legion may have stripped the timber components from their ramp at Machaerus for subsequent recycling at Masada, there is no evidence to support such a contention. Given the unfinished state of the ramp, the only timber available *in situ* would have been any hoarding provided as a revetment along the perimeter, as any timber corduroy along the top of the structure would not have been laid by the time of abandonment. Furthermore, it is difficult to see how the salvage party could have removed any structural timber from the body of the ramp (for which there is no surface indication in any event) without first demolishing the structure!

The siege mound at Cremna (*44*) is another large, dump-built structure extended by progressive piling of stone and earth, in this case, from west to east. This axis inclines gently upwards presenting an easy avenue of advance for the artillery (or the siege tower) that was positioned at the summit, whilst the south-facing aspect falls away at an angle of 18° and the north face presents an even steeper angle of 26°.[55] As a consequence of this sharp northern profile, the north-eastern perimeter of the mound is delimited by a curving dry-stone revetment, nowhere more than 1m in height (*45*), to limit any slippage of the mound core along this steep flank. This retaining work appears to have performed its function in a satisfactory manner as it is only at a few points that the wall has been breached by rubble fans.

The mound itself is comprised of ochre-coloured earth (in distinct contrast to the prevailing grey of the local limestone) and a rubble mix which has been transported to site. The artificiality of the structure is confirmed by a robbing pit at the summit dug to a depth of *c.*2m[56] revealing a homogenous (if loose) stone-and-earth matrix instead of bedrock. The surveyors also noted that the mound would appear to have been raised in two distinct stages, the first represented by a broad platform *c.*15m high extending for the full width of the structure. This was then augmented by a second stage comprising a cap *c.*10m high, which was sited directly opposite tower 6 on the city circuit. Although the addition of this second 'storey' may have been an integral part of the original design (i.e. to provide an elevated firing position for the artillery without the need for a siege tower), it is also possible that it may have been built in response to the raising of the enemy counter-mound.

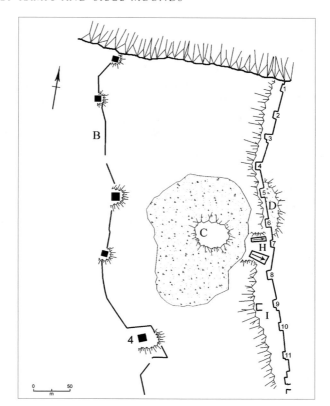

Right: 44 The siege mound and related features at Cremna with contravallation (B), siege mound (C), counter-mound (D), possible assault platforms (H), forward defensive work (I) and Roman artillery 'bastion' at turret 4

Below: 45 The revetment to the siege mound at Cremna

(ii) Timber-framed structures

In distinction to the 'simple' model of a piled earth ramp or mound relying upon its own (compacted) mass for basic stability, a separate category of work exists where timber support was employed as the major vehicle of structural strength. For convenience, the structures falling into this more sophisticated class are described here as 'timber-framed', whereas the method of construction may not always have involved the sort of lattice-work implied by this term. Of course, unless the *agger* in question was entirely composed of laid logs nailed (or bound) together, then these works would still have involved the dumping of a substantial volume of earth/stone packing retained within (and supported by) the timber carcass. The labour requirement for their construction would have been less time-consuming than for the preceding category as the timber-clad sides would have retained the fill, preventing any wasteful slumping, but the added burden of heavy-duty carpentry and/or pile-driving probably would have eroded any such advantage. A possible representation of a piled log assault ramp[57] appears on Trajan's Column.[58] This structure, comprised of cut timber with each row being laid at right-angles to the preceding course, is crowned by two open-backed galleries which would have served as covered approaches for the assault parties, with the nearside flank being protected by a form of timber stockade.

The ramp extended by the Theban-Lacedaemonian army at Plataea (429-427 BC) would appear to have been the first recorded example of this type of structure. We are specifically told that the engineers responsible for the Plataean ramp felled timber for their work on a nearby mountain and that the resulting logs were laid 'like lattice-work to form a sort of wall' on both sides of the ramp so that 'the mound might not spread too much'.[59] As the intervening space between these two 'walls' was then filled with earth, stone and assorted debris, it seems unlikely that that these timber elements were interlinked by any form of cross-bracing (i.e. were not a true 'lattice'), and, instead, would have resembled two parallel box ramparts acting as heavily reinforced revetments for the ramp edges.

If Silius Italicus is to be believed, then the siege mound raised at Capua (212-211 BC) would mark the first recorded appearance of these timber-framed structures in a Roman operation. Disregarding any possible anachronism, the mound allegedly raised here had sides made of planks arranged in a lattice,[60] a description that may, of course, have been a deliberate evocation of the Thucydidean account of the Plataean ramp. Despite the danger of reading too much into this brief explanation, the apparent choice of 'planks' over 'logs' not only implies the careful forethought and preparation that went into the construction process, but also hints at a lighter form of side-bracing than the crude bulk of a box rampart. If this was indeed the case, then the resulting arrangement might be reconstructed as a form of hoarding or screenwork reinforced by horizontal beams with either vertical or cross-bracing nailed into position to withstand the pressure of the fill.

Two of the mounds pushed forward by Trebonius at Massilia would appear to have employed a similar method of construction (although, again, this information is relayed to us in a poetical context). We are told that these huge embankments were built up out of a loose mixture of soil and brushwood, timber being required to compress and bind the soil by the carpentry of the sides and to prevent each mound from subsiding under the weight of the towers.[61] Once more, the reinforcement was provided by planks laid in a lattice[62] and that the defenders managed to fire and destroy one mound in the course of a sortie, suggests that timber must have formed a significant component of the work (the incendiary attack presumably consuming the lattice-work at the sides, causing the slumping of the fill and the destruction of the matériel emplaced at the summit).

The burning of one of Constantius' two mounds at Bezabde (AD 360), built to cover the advance of the great Persian ram captured at Carrhae, provides a further indication of how these structures were built. On this occasion, the defenders sallied out and inserted live coals into the joints of the mound, which, being built of the branches of various trees, rushes and bundles of cane, was quickly consumed.[63] Although this mound had been built up to a sufficient height to overtop the enemy wall, it was only intended to support two *ballistae* charged with clearing the parapets of combatants, explaining its relatively lightweight fabric. Indeed, from Ammianus' description, one might be tempted to reconstruct this 'mound' as a roughly formed scaffold filled with sufficiently coarse material that the sides did not have to be close-boarded. The resulting open-framed finish would have proved easy to sabotage, presenting the defenders with ample interstices for the introduction of combustible matter.

Several different techniques would seem to have been used for the raising of Titus' various ramps at Jerusalem, although the stress laid by Josephus on the shortage of timber does suggest that wood formed an invaluable component of the Roman works. Indeed, by the time of the final attack on the Temple compound, timber had to be transported from felling areas located over 100 stades/*c.*18km from the city, suggesting both the rate of consumption and the limitations of on-site scavenging for producing sufficient quantities of useful structural elements.

Of these various mounds and ramps, the best described[64] were those thrown up in the course of the first attack on the Antonia and the First wall. Although Josephus mentions four separate embankments (each being built by a different legion), these structures were clearly built as two paired sets. Those raised against the Antonia (by the Fifth and Twelfth legions) were sited only 20 cubits/*c.*10m apart, whilst those at the First wall (built by the Tenth and Fifteenth legions) were set only slightly further apart at 30 cubits/*c.*15m. A convincing suggestion has been put forward[65] that each of these paired sets reflects one ramp structure, with the separate 'embankments' representing the heavily reinforced sides of a single assault path (the intervening space presumably being filled with earth and rubble). This hypothesis is strengthened by the manner in which these ramps were destroyed: that thrown against the Antonia was successfully undermined in one operation (implying that this was a single, structurally contiguous work), whilst its First wall counterpart was consumed by flames after an incendiary attack directed against the engine housings fired the main body of the ramp (the speed with which the conflagration spread, again suggesting one structural entity). However, the possibility that each legion did raise its own individual ramp cannot be wholly discounted. After all, the competitive spirit that was fostered between units in the later stages of the campaign may well have had an earlier expression in a race to complete separate assault paths, and these may well have been built in close proximity so as to be mutually supportive and to benefit from a joint umbrella of artillery protection whilst construction was being undertaken.

46 Detail of the assault ramp at Masada with the timber elements arrowed

The different manner in which these two pairs of ramps were destroyed may also hint at some basic variation in their mode of construction, with the undermining of the first set perhaps reflecting a greater reliance upon an earth and stone fill compared to the second set, where a higher proportion of timber may have been used (a piled log assault path?) making the whole much more susceptible to incendiary attack.

Of our surviving assault ramps, only that at Masada has any evidence for the use of timber as a structural component. However, the contribution made by timber towards the overall stability of this work requires much more careful archaeological investigation before any firm conclusions can be drawn. The remains on the surface are not particularly prepossessing, comprising the projecting stubs of spindly timbers (which resemble branches rather than cut wood) seemingly driven into the ramp at *c.*30cm intervals (*46*). Analysis has revealed[66] that this timber was derived from either tamarisk or the few other trees that are found in the locality, suggesting that any imported timber would have been reserved for engine construction rather than for ramp support. It seems likely that the engineers here first proceeded to 'bench' the spur of bedrock on which the ramp was built by cutting a series of horizontal platforms at regular intervals along each flank. Thereafter, the timber box-revetment would have been installed on top of these steps and filled with rammed earth and small rubble. The ramp core could then have been deposited, secured on each side by this sequence of vertically stacked timber-framed boxes. Unfortunately, this supposition cannot be proved without excavation at site that penetrates to sufficient depth to reach bedrock.

Although there are frequent references to siege towers being deployed at the summit of both ramps and mounds there is little explicit mention as to how they were raised into position. Although it is possible that some of these towers were assembled *in situ* (which may explain the remark that the height of the towers at Avaricum rose alongside the daily increase in the size of the ramp),[67] most examples would appear to have been fabricated elsewhere and then moved into place. Only at Massilia can we conjecture that the towers were 'rolled' into position as a result of the mounds being pushed out from the opposite side of the valley that flanked the city walls so that a level platform could be maintained throughout. On other occasions, when the advantage of an elevated starting site was not available, the engineers would have needed to limit the steepness of the incline up which the engines were to be transported. As already noted, the profiles of the ramp at Machaerus and the mound at Cremna would seem to reflect this concern, although that the iron-clad tower and large ram employed at Masada could be moved up a ramp with a uniform gradient of at least 17°, does indicate that heavy equipment could be manoeuvred up relatively steep inclines. Of course, the deployment of the engines at Masada may have been assisted by the addition of a stone cap to the summit of the ramp, providing an operating platform and a reinforced base capable of absorbing both the weight of the machines and the recoil shock of repeated ram strikes (cf. the compacted 'crust' at Lachish). Unfortunately, the earthquake of 1927 has removed any subsisting trace of this feature, and as Josephus' account of its dimensions[68] can be considered prone to exaggeration,[69] we cannot establish the precise character of this reinforcing cap.

It is likely that the structures identified as 'Avaricum-style' ramps would have been of the timber-framed variety, as the burden of supporting combined function towers, covered assault corridors and forward artillery batteries on a wide frontage would have necessitated extensive buttressing to avoid structural failure. However, the vulnerability of such works to incendiary attack required that substantial cover be posted to resist hostile sallies (two legions being 'on standby' at Avaricum, whilst forward batteries, supported by both archers and cavalry on their flanks, protected the ramps advanced against the Third wall at Jerusalem). However, the frequency with which determined defenders still succeeded in setting fire to Roman ramps/mounds in spite of such precautionary expedients, does suggest that timber-supported works were particularly exposed to incendiary attack.

(d) Distance from the wall

The question of how close to an enemy wall to advance an *agger* was one largely determined by the functional role to be performed.

As siege mounds were meant to provide close-in artillery support, it would have been necessary to emplace the catapults (either with or without a tower) within range of the section of parapet to be cleared of defenders. The closer the pieces were sited to their target, then the greater the accuracy of the suppressive fire and the greater the possibility of causing actual structural damage to the enemy enceinte. In this regard, the siege mound at Cremna provides an excellent example, with the front base of the structure advanced to within 20m of the city wall allowing the artillery deployed at its summit to be less than 50m from the wall directly opposite. The actual damage inflicted on the wall fabric is particularly visible at towers 5 and 6 and along the battered curtain linking both positions (47), a testament to the kinetic power of heavy shot delivered at close range. The mound would also have been favourably placed to allow suppressive fire to be directed in support of attacks launched against the enemy wall further to the south, where the remains of what have been interpreted[70] as deliberately compacted assault platforms have been identified.

Although we have no specific information in this respect, the siege mounds advanced at Massilia were unlikely to have been sited in such close proximity to the enemy. After all, there was sufficient room in the interval between one mound and the enceinte to raise a brick redoubt and to extend a mobile, covered gallery from the same to the wall-base to allow sapping to proceed. Of course, had this forward face been properly revetted and clad in timber sheeting, then the front of the mound might have presented a vertical profile, but this must be a remote possibility given that the large stock of heavy artillery at the disposal of the defenders[71] would have exposed the work parties engaged in providing the necessary reinforcement to crippling casualties (penthouses, although adequate protection for pile-driving at the base, could not have covered men working on the upper surfaces of a mound 80ft high). It can also be assumed that the tower rolled into position along the embankment would have been recessed some considerable distance from the front edge of the structure, as the weight of a heavily-clad belfry would otherwise have threatened to destabilize the edges of the mound.

Assault ramps, on the other hand, had little option but to close on the enemy as they had to be in sufficient proximity to extend gangways across onto the wall-top and/or to allow the operation of the breaching engines. Although it might be thought that this would have involved a relatively straightforward (if arduous) process of piling up material until such time as it rested in sufficient depth against the enemy wall, a more methodical approach would generally have been called for. Indeed, the dangers of the former, haphazard procedure can be witnessed at the siege of Amida (AD 359), when the Roman counter-mound was piled against the inner face of the enceinte, but instead of buttressing the wall, the pressure of the earth caused its collapse outwards, bridging the *gap* between it and the Sassanian ramp.[72] Even though bringing about the collapse of the enemy circuit would have been a desirable objective for any assailant, the uncertainty of structural failure resulting from the simple physical pressure exerted by the mass of the ramp militated against the adoption of such a methodology. Furthermore, the attacker would himself have been exposed to heavy casualties at the moment of collapse (an unpredictable event) when the siege engines and the troops manning them would almost certainly have been lost as the ramp fell forward.

Apart from such concerns, another cogent reason for leaving a narrow interval between the ramp and the target would be to prevent any debris from collapsing on top of the rams.[73] This would have been particularly relevant where the ramp had been designed to cross an obstacle field so as to give the breaching engines access to the wall-base rather than an attack delivered at a higher level. In such circumstances, a substantial amount of masonry might be dislodged from a considerable height at the moment

47 The damaged town wall at Cremna from the Roman siege mound

that the breach was effected (i.e. as the whole face of the wall was brought down). Furthermore, if the ramp abutted the wall directly, then it might have proved easier for the defenders to disrupt the attack by dropping missiles (particularly combustibles) directly onto the structure or, indeed, to undertake sabotage by more subtle means. This latter option was exercised by the Plataeans when they opened a passageway through their defences to draw in the loose earth of the Theban–Lacedaemonian ramp. Although the ramp must therefore have rested against the defences directly, the fact that the besiegers subsequently attempted an incendiary attack by piling faggots 'into the space between the wall and the ramp',[74] suggests that only the lower courses of the structure in fact abutted the enceinte.

If a gap was to be left between the strike face of the ramp and the target as a result of these tactical reasons, then it would have been important to establish the precise point at which to halt construction if the interval space was not to be too broad to allow the assault preparations to proceed. The manner in which this calculation was determined is best illustrated from Josephus' account of Titus' attack on the Third wall at Jerusalem:

> the engineers measured the distance to the wall with lead and line, which they cast from the embankments – the only practicable method for men under fire from above – and finding that the battering-rams could reach it, they brought them up.[75]

Unfortunately, we have no details as to what would have been deemed an appropriate range at which either rams or assault gangways could have been effectively deployed. For the former, this would have depended upon the length of the pole, the method of operation (whether it was a balance ram or a simple propelled shaft) and the number of crew required to drive it. For the latter, the stability and the strength of the gangway would have limited the distance over which it could have been extended, and the objective of securing the wall-top with as strong a storming party as possible had to be tempered by technical constraints. After all, the hazards of attempting a bridging manoeuvre in a precipitate manner, either in the face of continuing resistance from the parapets or with too many troops, could easily result in failure. At Iotapata (AD 67), it was the defenders who rushed onto the gangways to engage the Romans and not *vice versa*, and when they were driven back, boiling fenugreek was poured onto the boards, making them too slippery to use.[76] Previously, at Metulum (35 BC), all four assault bridges thrown across from the two ramps collapsed under the weight of the troops attempting to cross over,[77] suggesting that in his eagerness to achieve a swift victory, Octavian had misjudged the width of the gap to be bridged.

Beyond Caesar's observation that his ramp at Avaricum was built up to such an extent that it was 'almost touching the enemy's wall',[78] there are few direct references that offer any clue as to the exact relationship between the terminal point of the ramp and the enemy circuit, and our archaeological examples can offer little additional assistance. As the stone platform at the summit of the Masada ramp has disappeared, and because the summit of the ramp itself presents a flattened, erosion-conditioned profile, it is impossible to offer any realistic assessment of the width of the intervening space. At Machaerus, calculations are hampered by the fact that the ramp was incomplete at the time of surrender, and, accordingly, the present day interval (*c*.15m-20m) between its eastern terminal and the base of the hill-top on which the fortress stands, may have been substantially closed by the time that the structure had become operational.

Unfortunately, this uncertainty is not likely to be resolved from the information currently at our disposal, and although experimental reconstruction might well provide some useful data in this regard, the feasibility of undertaking such a project is unlikely in view of the scale of work that would be necessary to obtain any meaningful results.

It must not be forgotten that the assault ramp was only one device that might be adopted to bring about the fall of a defended centre by direct means. Other initiatives (perhaps supported by the raising of a siege mound), such as escalades, the firing of the city gates or the infiltration of a small body of troops via some weak point in the enceinte do not involve siege works, but the alternative choice of a subterranean approach is clearly relevant here.

7

MINES

Instead of proceeding with an assault over or through the enemy wall, an assailant could also attempt an approach *under* the defences. The extension of underground galleries had two possible objectives: to undermine the wall circuit itself, causing a sectional collapse, or to gain surreptitious access to the interior, enabling a raiding party to seize a gate or length of wall allowing the entry of the remainder of the besieging force. Mines might also be dug for more indirect purposes, such as the Caesarian initiative to cut the feeder channels to the spring at Uxellodunum (51 BC), or to counter attempts by the defenders to sabotage the progress of ramp/mound construction. Of course, mines were not practicable where the terrain was unfavourable (e.g. where the bedrock was too hard) or where the target was protected by a deep moat (particularly if water-filled).

Mining operations should also be distinguished from efforts to sap the enemy wall as although the object may have been similar in both cases (to achieve the collapse of a length of curtain or a projecting tower), the latter process did not involve any field work or construction. As a simple act of stone leverage or removal carried out under the cover of a *testudo* or some form of penthouse, sapping does not fall within the parameters of this book.

THE ROMAN USE OF MINING

Although the use of mines might seem an obvious expedient of siege warfare, references to their employment in Persian and Greek contexts are relatively few.[1] Mines do, however, feature in four separate Roman siege operations up to the fall of Veii, although it is probably significant that these initiatives were launched either against Fidenae (620s, 496-494 and 436-435 BC) or Veii itself (396 BC).[2] On all but one of these occasions (the second Fidenate siege) these tunnels were driven under the walls for infiltration purposes. Given the symbolic significance of the seizure of Veii, it seems likely that the tactics that prevailed there would have been vividly preserved in the collective memory, and it is always possible that these familiar events were extrapolated into the deeper past to explain the capture of Fidenae. However, it should also be noted that the soft tufa that underlies both Veii and Fidenae would have been eminently suitable for mining operations, and existing cavities in the rock (tombs, storage spaces, etc.) might have expedited the process of excavation, particularly as the proximity of both cities to Rome would have given the besiegers a detailed knowledge of their environs. Accordingly, as tunnelling would have been technically feasible at both sites, especially when the main aim was to obtain secret entry via a relatively simple gallery, we cannot dismiss out of hand the early use of these techniques.[3]

Despite the success at Veii, the idea of taking a defended centre by infiltration from a hidden gallery does not appear to have enjoyed wide currency, and on those rare occasions when a Roman commander ordered an underground attack, it was usually for the purpose of undermining the enemy enceinte. As these attempts rarely appear to have been successful, it is not surprising that mining was viewed as a strategy of last resort.[4] This is not to say that the Romans were poor miners (the complex works driven under the walls of Ambracia in 189 BC demonstrate competence in both the planning and excavation of tunnels)[5] but that the method of attack itself was too time-consuming (and ultimately, too uncertain) to contemplate unless all other expedients had been attempted.

During the first century BC, a small revival occurs in the employment of mines with most of these initiatives seeking to bring about the subsidence of the enemy circuit (as at the Piraeus, 86 BC or at Avaricum, 52 BC).[6] Sometimes these galleries were also dug to counter mines sunk by the besieged to delay the advance of Roman ramps (again at the Piraeus and, possibly, at the stronghold of the Sotiates, 56 BC)[7] or for specialist purposes (as in the case of Caesar's adits at Uxellodunum).[8] Quite frequently, the intersection of mines and counter-mines would result in fierce battles below ground, leading to the adoption of unusual measures by the defenders to drive the Roman pioneers from their works (as at Ambracia or Themiscyra, 72 BC).[9]

The fact that Josephus makes no mention of mines during the Flavian suppression of the Jewish Revolt (except those dug by the besieged), probably means that the tactic was no longer regarded as a useful or relevant option. Indeed, it is interesting to note that during the staff conference called by Titus after the failure of his initial attack on the Antonia, there was no mention of mining as a serious alternative to the various reductive methods that were actually discussed.[10] The general absence of references to the aggressive use of mines after the first century BC, suggests that imperial generals regarded this technique with even less favour than their republican predecessors.

That Vegetius was still able to recommend[11] underground approaches to a potential assailant, may perhaps be connected to the isolated (but undoubtedly well-publicized) success achieved by Julian at Maiozamalcha.[12] This operation involved a reversion to the antique device of the gallery as a conduit for the infiltration of a picked body of men who then overran the defenders from within, a tactic that had not been employed since the capture of Veii. It is not improbable that this action was consciously intended to echo that past triumph, with Julian casting himself as the embodiment of ancient virtue, the resurrection of which might 'save' the empire from its ignoble descent. Notwithstanding the fortunate outcome of the incident at Maiozamalcha, this resort to tunnelling should probably be regarded as a one-off curiosity.

FORM AND STRUCTURE

(a) The tunnels

Mining would only have been practicable where the underlying geology was conducive to the excavation of galleries. Although it may have been within the technical capacity of an assailant to drive a shaft through hard bedrock, the consequent delay and the probability that secrecy would have been compromised by the noise of tunnelling, would have made this an unprofitable exercise. Equally, where the soil was too friable, so that the workings would have been exposed to the constant threat of collapse, alternative methods of attack would have been preferred. The significance of geological factors is made explicit when Curtius makes the specific observation that Alexander used mines at Gaza (332 BC) because the light and easily worked soil made a hidden approach feasible.[13] Furthermore, the nature of the strata encountered beneath ground might also determine the alignment of any tunnel actually dug, with the change in course in one of the galleries at Uxellodunum seemingly being prompted by the desire to follow a comparatively soft bed of lias.[14] However, a degree of difficulty might sometimes be tolerated: in Philip of Macedon's efforts before Lamia (191 BC), mines were advanced notwithstanding the toughness of the bedrock (although Livy's report[15] of the episode may have been coloured by his wish to contrast Macedonian industry with the sluggish performance of the consular army before Locrian Heraclea).

It is reasonable to expect that the character of the tunnels extended by the Romans would have reflected the task in hand. Galleries intended to bring down a section of wall needed to be sufficiently capacious to allow the props and the necessary combustible matter (sulphur, hemp and pitch was used at the Piraeus) to be carried along to a firing chamber which had to be broad enough to cause a collapse on a relatively extensive front. On the other hand, tunnels built to allow a storming party access to the interior of the target could take the form of narrow galleries without any further elaboration, although the provision of reinforcing pit props may have forced the engineers to open wider passageways where the geology so demanded. Although this supposition appears weakened by the evidence from Dura Europos, where the gallery described as the 'mine of attack' was wider than the others, the specialized circumstances of this operation may account for the discrepancy (see below).

It is doubly unfortunate that the only *offensive* Roman mine for which we have any physical evidence is that uncovered by Napoleon III at Uxellodunum, given that the excavations were poorly reported and that the tunnel was intended to perform an unusual function in severing the enemy water supply.[16] Over its re-opened length, the gallery, once cleared of its thick deposits of water-deposited silts, was found to be arch-shaped having a height of 1.8m and a width of 1.5m, with its vertical pit props and horizontal roof bracing being preserved as a result of petrification.[17] No section diagrams were published by the excavators and no information was provided as to either the dimensions of, or the intervals between, the timber reinforcing elements. As previously noted, the tunnel did not head directly towards its target but sought to take the line of least resistance by following the most easily worked stratum. Considering that the mine was extended for the purpose of diverting header springs, the reported height and width of the gallery would seem quite generous. However, as these measurements presumably would have reflected the smallest working space necessary for driving forward an adit efficiently, the dimensions of the Uxellodunum tunnel can be extrapolated more generally to obtain a crude impression of the minimum specification for a Roman mine.

The survival of the four tunnels dug by the Cypriot defenders to sabotage the Persian ramp at Palaepaphos also provide some useful comparative data. Here, the careful excavation of tunnel 1 revealed that the gallery had been started at a level c.2.8m below the base of the city wall and sloped down to a maximum depth of 4m below the ground surface, whilst its dimensions varied between 1.2m-1.7m in width and 1.7m-2.3m in height.[18] Tunnel 4 was somewhat slighter, having a width of 1.1m-1.5m and a height of 1.4m-1.8m, although it too was dug in a similar manner, 'with nearly vertical side walls and a roughly concave roof'.[19] Both these examples had niches cut in their side walls containing lamps which were clearly intended as illumination bays for the pioneers. An added refinement was provided at the mouth of tunnel 1, where retaining walls prevented any upcast from trickling back into the works. The hazards of the operation can be suggested from the unfinished condition of tunnel 2, which the excavator believed to have been abandoned as a result of a roof collapse.[20] There was no indication of any timber revetment preserved *in situ* along the passageways, suggesting that the defenders carried out their counter-mining without installing any bracing. However, the terminal chambers of both tunnels 1 and 3 did have mud-brick piers that presumably acted to support the roof at the point where the firing of the ramp was to have taken place.[21]

Even more directly relevant are the three Persian mines (and one Roman counter-mine) uncovered at Dura Europos.[22] Each of the mines sunk by the Persians would appear to have been designed to fulfil a different purpose and their respective characters vary markedly. The first of these (tunnel 1)[23] comprised a relatively straight approach work that was aimed at the south-west angle of tower 19 and then turned sharply to the south to run under the adjoining curtain (unfortunately, the dimensions of the work are not reported). When the charge laid in the firing chamber was set alight, the tower dropped vertically 2.5m into the cavity. Had it not been for the reinforcing batter of the external *glacis*, it is likely that both the corner of the tower and the adjacent 15m of wall would have collapsed outwards, causing a major breach. The second tunnel (tunnel 2), although also dug for undermining purposes, does not appear to have been excavated with a breach in mind as a primary objective. Rather, tunnel 2, although 'a narrow, twisting' affair 'unsupported by wood and scarcely the height of a man',[24] was aimed at the middle of the north face of tower 14 and, thereafter, cut beneath the north, east and west foundations of that structure, making sabotage the most likely intention. At the point that it approached the foundations, the mine broadened out and timber supports were added to brace the wider space. Here also, a narrow side-branch was provided which ran the short distance to a nearby ravine, where it opened out onto the sheltered side bank. The excavators speculated that this was probably intended to provide a supplementary air intake so that a draught could be stimulated when the combustible material was lit, allowing the resulting fire to burn all the more fiercely.[25] Given that tower 14 could have delivered murderous flanking fire against the nearby Persian assault ramp, it is reasonable to follow the excavator's hypothesis that tunnel 2 was designed to disable this threatening artillery position before work could commence on raising the *agger*.[26]

The last of the Persian tunnels (tunnel 3), located just a few metres to the south of the assault ramp, penetrated beneath the enceinte and rose to the surface behind the earthen revetment that reinforced the city wall on its inner face. This was clearly intended as 'mine of attack' (to follow the excavator's terminology)[27] and presumably would have served to enable a column of Persian troops to enter the city simultaneously with an assault launched from the ramp. This tunnel was considerably wider (at *c*.3m) than its fellows, so much so that the excavator claims that it would have been sufficiently broad to allow a column of men to march four abreast.[28] However, it may well be that the Persian priority lay in gaining access to the city with the maximum number of troops in shortest possible time rather than a surreptitious infiltration (certainly it would have been very difficult to disguise the construction of such a large gallery). Indeed, the signs of a conflagration at the mouth of the tunnel where it debouched into the city, as well as a skeleton left *in situ*, may well suggest that the defenders had calculated the point of penetration and had prepared an ambush for the enemy storming party. It is worth pointing out that despite the scale of this tunnel, it was not furnished with any timber bracing except in its final stages after it had commenced its climb to the surface. Presumably this would suggest that the soil beneath the city wall (and its earth dump reinforcement) had been compacted by the weight of the superstructure and was sufficiently stable to allow a wide, open adit to be driven through it, support only becoming necessary in the unconsolidated strata within the urban area.

This open construction technique can be readily contrasted with the form taken by the Roman counter-mine driven to intercept tunnel 1. A perfectly preserved section near the north-east angle of tower 19 revealed a gallery *c*.1.6m wide with sides made of 'two lines of round hardwood posts 0.10m–0.11m in diameter and about 2m in length sawed straight at the two ends. The distance [i.e. the width of tunnel] between the line of posts was about 1.2m and they were implanted in the earth to depths varying from 0.25–0.37m.'[29] These posts were set along the sides of the tunnel at an average spacing of 0.28m and they supported a roof of strong planks up to 4cm thick covering the width of the gallery. These details are worth repeating as these unique conditions of preservation have presented us with detailed evidence for at least one method of gallery construction. The existence of a wooden ceiling above the side props suggests that the Roman sappers were sufficiently confident of their mining abilities to drive a tunnel through loosely consolidated soil (cf. the more stable environment in the Persian 'mine of attack') and that these planks were sturdy enough to prevent any roof collapse.

(b) Practical considerations

Perhaps the most important consideration for any assailants engaged in mining, was to maintain as much secrecy as possible regarding their plans. After all, if the defenders received intelligence to indicate that the besiegers were undertaking underground approaches, then their counter-measures might include sinking their own galleries to intercept the advancing tunnel or carrying out some other blocking work.[30] Even more disastrous from the besiegers' point of view, would be the betrayal of a gallery extended under the enemy walls for the purpose of surreptitious entry. Any forewarning would have allowed the defenders to prepare an ambush for the raiding party as it broke out from the tunnel. Accordingly, for as long as mines have been employed as a method of attack, their builders have adopted various ruses to disguise the progress of their work or to deceive the besieged as to their actual intentions.

That such stratagems were employed even in the deep past has been suggested for the Israelite siege of Jericho,[31] where the marching of the host around the city and the blowing of trumpets, might have been a deliberate ploy to distract the defenders from the noise of the tunnelling that would eventually cause the collapse of their walls. It would seem that the Romans also understood the value of concealing their mining activities from the enemy, as Servilius' efforts against Fidenae (436-435 BC) suggest. Here, a continuous series of attacks was maintained from all directions against the town walls, keeping the defenders off-balance until the work of excavating a tunnel directly under the citadel was completed, while as a further precaution, the mine was commenced from the 'least guarded' flank of the target.[32] Similarly, at Veii, when Camillus was informed that his gallery had been finished and merely awaited opening, he ordered the launch of a general attack to draw the enemy's attention to their walls and to pin them in position.[33] Meanwhile at Ambracia, as a specific measure of last resort as Polybius notes,[34] Fulvius undertook the construction of a secret tunnel, concealing his efforts from the defenders by extending it from a covered shed running parallel to the enemy circuit over a distance of c.100 yards. Unfortunately, although these precautions prevented the besieged from divining his intention to start with, the consul ruined the surprise value of this endeavour by failing to arrange for the subtle disposal of the spoil from the workings. The mounting upcast was soon noticed, alerting the defenders to their predicament.

One way to keep defenders ignorant of the existence of a mine would be to begin the work at a considerable distance from the target. Thus when Darius undertook his attack on Chalcedon (late sixth century BC), his engineers commenced their approach from the slopes of the Aphasius Hill, a full 15 stades from the city wall![35] However, unless one was prepared for considerable delay, or had a sufficiently large workforce, then most mines would have been started as close as possible to the defences. Although this risked compromising security unless undertaken behind some covering work,[36] the shorter excavation time may have allowed the work to be completed before the enemy had the time to devise suitable counter-measures.

At Dura, both tunnels 1 and 2 were started at a distance of c.40m from their targets, and although this meant that they would have been within easy range of the artillery and archers posted on the enemy circuit, precautions were taken to limit the effect of such interdiction. The entrance to tunnel 1 was masked by a heap of earth 3.65m in height, 28m in length and 16m in width,[37] presumably representing the upcast from the workings which, when complemented by screens, would have served to shield the pioneers. Such an obvious mound would have been noticed by the defenders (allowing them sufficient time in which to prepare their counter-mine), although on such a flat plain the assailants would have found it very difficult to conceal their intentions without engaging in extensive deception (such as dummy mine-heads). The entrance to tunnel 2 was much more effectively concealed by driving the gallery into the side of a ravine out of sight of the defenders. This blind spot allowed the mine to be built in secrecy by enabling the work parties to move up under cover and by permitting the spoil to be disposed of in a controlled manner.

Other important considerations were the competence and condition of the miners charged with advancing the tunnel, as these factors would determine the speed of the process. Working underground involves hard labour in less than ideal conditions, and unless the troops were specifically trained in the role, it would be unrealistic to expect that individuals could have sustained an intensive work-rate for very long. This impression is supported by the limited information that we have regarding Roman mining. At Veii for example, Camillus divided the men responsible for the tunnelling into six different groups who worked six-hour shifts both day and night, so that whilst one group laboured at the mine face, a second was presumably removing the spoil.[38] This arrangement would have allowed the pioneers a 12-hour break between their respective shifts. Similarly, at Ambracia, Fulvius split his men into work details that were then rotated on a 24-hour duty roster.[39]

As for the question of competence, it was clearly advantageous to have men with considerable knowledge of underground workings and the presence of auxiliary infantry from mining districts such as Thrace might have improved the performance of the besieging army. This is certainly true in reverse, when our sources sometimes make the observation that certain opponents proved particularly adept at driving tunnels under (or into) the Roman workings because of their 'natural' expertise in such matters (the copper-mining experience of the Sotiates, 56 BC, was cited as the reason for their attempted sabotage of the advancing ramp from beneath).[40] However, it is also interesting to note that Julian's mine at Maiozamalcha was completed by legionaries assigned to the task as the original miners had been insufficiently attentive to their duties.[41]

Apart from the possible employment of specialist miners, a siege commander who had opted to infiltrate the target by means of a mine needed to ensure that the assault troop charged with operating behind enemy lines was capable of performing its allocated role. To this extent, Camillus detailed a selected force to emerge from the gallery at Veii and to open the town gates from within.[42] Even more specifically, the names and status of the men who broke out of Julian's mine at Maiozamalcha have been recorded (Exsuperius/Superantius, 'a famous man in the legion of the Victores', followed by the tribune Magnus and the *primicerius notariorum* Jovianus)[43] so that we have a vivid confirmation that the best and bravest men under Julian's command were assigned this dangerous task.

Mines might have provided the classical authors with a suitable tableau upon which to re-enact some of the most dramatic incidents of siege warfare, but it should be acknowledged that their material contribution to Roman operations was extremely limited. Not only were they employed comparatively rarely, but the success rate of those actually dug was scarcely commensurate with the labour actually invested. However, even if mining may not have been commonly employed in the conventional repertoire of Roman siege techniques, the early references to its use suggest nonetheless that this was the first technically informed reductive method to be employed by the nascent Roman state.

8

MISCELLANEOUS ENGINEERING WORKS

An important attribute of the successful siege commander was the ability to adopt a flexible approach to the challenges confronting him. This not only entailed a preparedness to adapt his chosen siege strategy in response to changing circumstances, but also a willingness to entertain unconventional stratagems where appropriate. Alongside this capacity for spontaneity, a prudent commander needed to ensure that he had made adequate provision for the various indirect functions that allowed the seamless prosecution of his operation. Both these aspects of generalship are reflected in this final category that covers works designed to overcome specific tactical problems as well as measures undertaken to improve the efficiency of the siege system.

SITE-SPECIFIC SOLUTIONS

In the course of operations directed against coastal centres, an assailant might undertake large-scale works either to assist with the approach to the target, or to isolate the same from ship-borne reinforcements and supplies. We have already seen how the former objective might be satisfied by the extension of an existing access corridor,[1] but on occasion an entirely new avenue of advance might be constructed. One of the earliest examples of this approach can be seen at Drepanum (247 BC) where the consul seized an offshore islet and filled in the shallow strait between it and the mainland so that he might launch his attack against the weakest section of the city walls.[2] But perhaps the clearest exemplification of this type of work can be seen in the course of the Caesarian campaign directed against the coastal strongholds of the Veneti (56 BC) where the range and power of the tides defeated conventional attacks both by land and sea. The solution adopted in each case was to hold the sea at bay by means of a massive mole built up to the level of the defenders' walls,[3] so that the resulting structures effectively fulfilled the roles of both causeway and assault ramp. This labour intensive and time consuming expedient was successful in reducing individual centres, but the campaign could not be won by such tactics alone, as the defenders simply carried out a naval evacuation of their personnel and portable property as soon as the embankment directly threatened their walls.

The first Roman use of siege works as a harbour-blocking device occurred during the siege of Lilybaeum (250-249 BC). Here, to prevent blockade-runners from slipping in and out of the anchorage, moles were to be extended across the entrance to the port. However, the depth of the water and the scouring action of the tide defeated the efforts of the besiegers, notwithstanding their use of the novel contrivance of artillery-delivered rubble as part of the infilling process.[4] A limited success was, however, achieved when a solid bank was established on what had been a section of reef, and a Carthaginian vessel that ran foul of the same was salvaged by the besiegers and outfitted as an interceptor. Despite the failure of this initiative, when Claudius Pulcher assumed command in the second year of the siege he earned the scorn of Diodorus Siculus by seeking to reconstruct the 'jetties and the barriers in the sea', although predictably enough, once again 'the sea hurled all to bits'.[5]

A more successful attempt to deny an anchorage to blockade-runners was undertaken by Scipio Aemilianus during his siege of Carthage. This Roman embankment was an enormous undertaking being built of heavy stones 'so that it might not be washed away by the waves', and, if Appian is to be believed, its breadth above the surface amounted to 24ft whilst its base on the seabed was four times as wide![6] Although this structure proved resistant to the tides and managed to seal off the enemy harbour, the Carthaginians cut an alternate channel to the sea to restore contact with the outside world.

Caesar also made an effort to close off a harbour mouth when he sought to trap Pompey's army at Brundisium (49 BC).[7] This was another ambitious scheme as although the entrance was not particularly wide, the water in the centre of the channel was very deep and subject to strong rip-tides. Accordingly, the moles that were extended out from either shore lost all structural cohesion as soon as they reached the deeper water. The Caesarians then extemporized a replacement barrier comprising 30ft square rafts secured at each corner by a separate anchor, which were lashed together and affixed to the ends of the breakwaters. These rafts were then covered in soil to present a continuous causeway crowned with mantlets and screens, and on every fourth raft a two-storey tower was raised to defend the structure against naval attack. This remarkable work was completed in a very short period of time demonstrating the versatility of the troops responsible for its construction and the imagination of their commander. Unfortunately, the Pompeian response was also decisive, with the fitting out of merchantmen equipped with artillery towers that succeeded in breaking through the Caesarian pontoons, losing two vessels in the process.

Perhaps the most successful of all these works of coastal blockade were the measures instituted at Gesoriacum (AD 293). In the course of his operation against this rebel fleet-base, Constantius Chlorus ordered that the anchorage be denied the enemy by the driving of piles into the seabed reinforced with boulders. This work was clearly constructed with considerable difficulty as the problems caused by the ebb and flow of the tide were specifically mentioned by the panegyrist.[8] In all likelihood, a reconstruction of Constantius' barrier would resemble a stout palisade line of stakes (probably driven into the seabed at an acute angle) across the harbour mouth. The boulders would not have projected above the surface nor would they have acted as a submerged reef, but would have had the specific task of weighing down the anchor points of the piles, protecting the same against the scouring of the tide and any enemy attempt to drag them out of position.

Another broad context for the construction of specific engineering works would be those measures designed to divert the water supply of the defenders. Cutting any artificial water channel would have been an obvious preliminary to most siege operations (e.g. when the partisans of Gordian III sought to deny Maximinus' supporters holding out in the Praetorian Camp at Rome, AD 238, by diverting 'the camp water supply into new channels by cutting and blocking up the pipes leading into the camp'),[9] but more ambitious projects were also attempted from time to time. Thus, in the course of his operation against Isaura Vetus (75 BC), Servilius forced the issue by diverting a nearby stream which formed the main water supply for the defenders.[10] Somewhat more explicit information is to hand regarding the Caesarian initiative at Dyrrachium to deny the Pompeians ready access to water. Here, efforts were made to divert or to block all the streams and channels that ran down to the sea, damming all the defiles between the hills by sinking piles into the ground and heaping up earth.[11] Although the construction of these barrages did cause considerable distress in the ranks of the besieged, they did not prove decisive as the Pompeians sank wells to alleviate their shortage. Presumably the ponding effect of the dams would also have created some inconvenience for the besiegers as the flooding of the valleys behind their lines would have disrupted their most obvious routes of communication and supply.

The Pompeian response may have been influenced by their commander's experience in Armenia (67 BC) when he occupied a favourable hill-top position recently abandoned by Mithridates because of an apparent lack of water.[12] However, Pompey had previously noted the lushness of vegetation on the slopes as well as the channels that scored the hillside, and he was convinced that there were sufficient springs in the locality. The wells that were subsequently dug by his men duly produced a copious supply of water and the Roman commander was then well placed to maintain a proper siege of the secondary position occupied by the Mithridatic army.

Apart from fulfilling the water requirements of the defenders, rivers could also act as corridors along which supplies and reinforcements might be infiltrated into the besieged centre. Decimus Brutus, locked up within Mutina (44-43 BC) by Mark Antony's close investment, managed to maintain contact with the relief armies by inscribing messages on rolled sheets of lead that were then entrusted to a diver who swam downstream at night.[13] Furthermore, when the stock of salt within the city reached a critical level, it proved feasible to pack replacement supplies in jars and to float them down the river.[14] Such possibilities inspired Scipio's decision to bar the Duero (*colour plate 17*) against Numantine re-provisioning and raiding parties by raising a tower on each bank and by suspending a boom across the river comprising timbers studded with blades and spearheads.[15] The flailing action that resulted from the current keeping these logs in constant rotation dissuaded the defenders from making further use of the river. A simpler (but equally effective) deterrent was devised by Brutus at Xanthus (42 BC) where nets were placed across the river to catch any escapee attempting to swim downstream.[16] The added refinement of attaching bells to the guy ropes, alerted the besiegers to the fate of any individual unfortunate enough to become entangled within this obstruction.

SUPPORTING WORKS

The second broad category of works discussed here are those intended to fulfil essential supporting functions. Whilst these may not have had a direct impact upon the defenders or their capacity to resist, their contribution to the final success of the operation might still be considered decisive.

Perhaps the best illustration of this type of siege work can be seen in the 'engineering yard' or *Baulager* – a distinct area in which the various craft processes associated with the assembly of siege paraphernalia and the manufacture of war matériel might be concentrated. Such provision would make operational sense whenever a long-term operation was anticipated or where the issue was to be determined by the deployment of large-scale engines. A *fabrica* would not always be required in such circumstances, as the siege train might sometimes transport the necessary machines in a pre-assembled state without the need for further engineering intervention (as in the case of the great ram abandoned by the Persians at Carrhae, which Constantius had dragged[17] to Bezabde, AD 360, to assist with his assault). However, any requirement for iron-clad siege towers or for the provision of stone artillery missiles, for example, would generally have been satisfied by on-site assembly/manufacture, and that the place of production (certainly for the heavier pieces) would have been as close as possible to their eventual point of deployment. In view of this latter consideration, it would be sensible to furnish the assembly area with some form of enclosure so as to provide some element of security against any hostile sally.

One of the earliest purpose-built armaments complexes was Scipio Africanus' arsenal at Utica (204-203 BC) where new engines were manufactured by local artisans who had been interned specifically for this purpose.[18] Similarly, whenever we learn of new siege equipment being prepared *in situ* (as before Gytheum, 195 BC or Ambracia, 189 BC),[19] it seems reasonable to suppose that some form of assembly area was set aside, although it remains unclear whether this need always have comprised a separate compound (as opposed to an assigned zone within an existing encampment). Perhaps the clearest archaeological evidence for a formal 'engineering yard' can be found at Masada, where a levelled platform, *c.*40m x 30m, was annexed to the back of the circumvallation, just to the south of the Λευκη.[20] On the other three sides, this was surrounded by a wall with a gauge of 1.4m (only slightly narrower than the circumvallation itself), and its interior contained signs of industrial activity in the form of 'working hearths'.[21] Although subsequent commentators have sought to downplay the interpretation of this feature as a deliberate *fabrica*, preferring to explain it instead as a concentration camp for the corvée labour,[22] the original hypothesis remains a far more convincing proposition.[23]

Ensuring proper communications between the different sectors of his siege system would also have been a significant concern for any commander, and achieving this objective would often have involved a substantial engineering effort. One example of an initiative to connect two topographically distinct sections of line, can be recognized at Masada. Here, the eastern circuit of the circumvallation lay at the foot of the mesa on which the fortress stood, whilst the western part was raised on the cliff-edge forming

48 The communications path at Masada climbing the escarpment north-west of camp D

the rim of the rift valley, at least another 100m higher. In order to link both sections of his line, Silva undertook the construction of an important artery carefully engineered to climb the scarp to the west of camp D. This narrow, zig-zag path (*48*), was never more than 2m wide, and although its sharp bends and steep gradients would have made it impractical for anything other than mules and porters, it would have sufficed to allow the movement of supplies from the putative depots on the eastern front to the isolated bases in the west. Another far less dramatic roadway would appear to have been set immediately behind the rampart of the contravallation on the plaine de Grésigny at Alesia.[24] This was revealed as a layer of compacted gravel *c.*3.5m wide and 10cm thick, similar in character to a road-bed recovered from one of the camps on the circuit. Such a roadway would have enabled the rapid transfer of men and equipment between any section of line that was threatened with an overwhelming enemy attack, and it is only surprising that similar lateral communication routes have not been found elsewhere on the Caesarian circuit.

THE BRICK STRUCTURES AT MASSILIA

The unusual brick-built structures raised by Trebonius at Massilia (49 BC) deserve to be described separately because of their uniquely sophisticated character.

The first of these was a tower built 'beneath the wall' (but as a gallery was later extended from this to the base of the city wall, it is more likely that the structure was built adjacent to, or immediately in advance of, the main siege mound) to serve as 'a stronghold and place of retreat' for the legionaries working in this area.[25] This was a square-shaped 30ft x 30ft brick building with walls 5ft thick, which provided shelter during the heaviest enemy sorties and which allowed the troops to rally and, subsequently, counter-attack, at the most opportune moment. Although this was originally just a low blockhouse, it was quickly appreciated that raising the height of the structure would convey immediate advantages (49). Accordingly, despite sorties and heavy artillery fire directed against them, the soldiers added a floor at first storey level, making sure that the beams of the same were sunk into the thickness of the wall and did not project externally (where they would be vulnerable to incendiaries).[26] This floor was covered with bricks and clay to make the planks invulnerable to fire-missiles and a further layer of mattresses was added to the same to cushion the impact of more conventional projectiles. A framework was then raised above the floor with projecting horizontal joists from which screens were hung to deflect enemy missiles, and additional rope 'fenders' were suspended from the main vertical timbers. All these precautions allowed the skin of the brick wall to be built up progressively until the intended height of the second storey was reached whereupon the new 'roof' was raised into place by an ingenious system of leverage. This process was repeated several times until the besiegers had possession of a tower with a total of six storeys mounting a large number of anti-personnel engines for which apertures had been liberally provided. Although this structure was eventually destroyed in the course of a treacherous sortie in breach of truce, it seems remarkable that such a tall tower could have remained upright for so long. After all, the weight of the superstructure combined with the men and equipment posted in it, could scarcely have been commensurate with the original design parameters (the foundations, if any, would only have been provided for the initial blockhouse).

The usefulness of this structure was soon demonstrated when a mobile gallery (with a pitched tile roof and brick upperworks and with elaborate water jets maintaining a constant spray of water over the whole ensemble) was pushed into position to link the tower with the base of the enemy wall.[27] Thus, not only did the tower provide the anchor point for the gallery, but also the suppressive fire directed from it (presumably supplementing the barrage mounted from the siege mound) allowed the sappers to proceed unhindered with the task of dislodging the basal stones from one of the enemy bastions.

After the surprise sally which destroyed the mobile gallery, the brick tower and the main siege mound, Trebonius refused to be disheartened and proceeded to construct a replacement for the last of these. As all the trees within Massiliote territory had already been cut down to provide for his earlier works, the Caesarian commander had recourse 'to a novel kind' of building 'that no-one had heard of before'.[28] This comprised a roofed structure of approximately the same width as the previous mound, but with side-walls made out of brick, 6ft thick. Internally, this was reinforced by cross beams and, where the roof timber seemed weak, by intervening piles. The roof itself was protected by clay-covered hurdles which served to frustrate any hostile incendiary attack and openings were left in the flanks of the structure to allow counter-sorties to be launched. Clearly, given its hollow construction, this new work cannot be thought of as either a siege

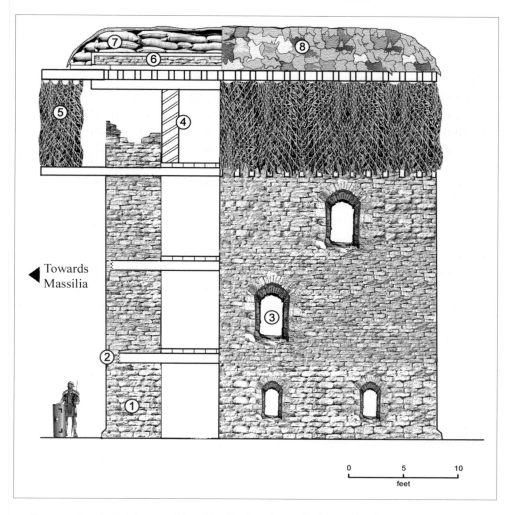

Towards
Massilia

0   5   10
feet

49 Constructing the brick tower (1) at Massilia: floor beams built into the wall (2), apertures for
catapults (3), leverage system to raise the roof (4), hanging fenders (5), brick and clay cladding (6),
mattress cushion (7) and postulated hide cover (8)

mound or as an assault ramp, and as its purpose was to serve as a protected corridor for
the advance of both men and equipment towards the enemy wall, it would be more
sensible to view this as a unique form of fixed gallery.

Whereas the brick structures at Massilia evidence a particularly sophisticated form
of adaptation by Roman combat engineers, the ingenuity of this initiative may be
considered characteristic of the flexible thinking that was so often displayed by those
charged with the responsibility of prosecuting a difficult siege. This is not to say that
the resulting formula would always be crowned with success, but that commanders
were prepared to entertain such unusual tactics betokens a confident reliance upon the
capabilities of the troops under their control.

CONCLUSIONS

In the course of this book, the Roman response to the challenges of 'fortress-war' has been outlined, at least insofar as the structural components of the siege system are concerned. This concentration on the topic of siege works has allowed us to observe how Roman practice would appear to have varied over time, with the changing emphasis of reductive approaches being reflected in the chosen ensemble of siege works actually deployed. This emphasis would be far harder to ascertain from a study of the engines and supporting équipage of the siege train where there was much less variation in the range of machines and housings used from the third century BC onwards.

It is appropriate to provide a summary of the general trajectory of development in this concluding section.

The earliest campaigns of the Roman state took the form of relatively brief expeditions mounted in the most favourable months of the year against nearby towns. Sieges would have been loosely enforced affairs prosecuted from the security of a blockade camp, although the effort of maintaining the field army in fixed positions at any remove from Rome itself, would have promoted attempts to force the issue either by escalade or by the subtler intercession of bribery or a *ruse de guerre*. As we have seen, the mythic quality of the siege of Veii may have distorted the accuracy of our accounts of this episode, but the extended quality of the operation and the establishment of winter quarters can probably be taken to presage a new phase of professionalism stemming from an improved organizational capacity allowing the development of more sophisticated siege techniques. Certainly, by the time of the First Punic War, Roman resources had expanded to a sufficient degree to enable large field armies to operate deep within enemy territory and to embark upon ambitious programmes of city-taking involving the employment of siege works in an increasingly systematic manner.

The purposive determination of the Roman state, demonstrated at several times of crisis during the course of the Hannibalic War, was also reflected in a number of important sieges at this time. Thus the investments of Capua and Syracuse were maintained (notwithstanding enemy pressure applied on other fronts) in an impressive display of application made possible by the careful organization of supply lines and the elaborate precautions taken to protect the besieging forces. These sophisticated operations may be regarded as templates for later planned operations at Carthage and Numantia.

Although there were several well-conducted investments in the intervening years, perhaps the ultimate expression of Roman siegecraft can be found in Caesar's Gallic campaign. Here, the combination of veteran troops well-versed in field fortification techniques and an imaginative and flexible commander, resulted in the construction of a series of elaborate siege works which were instrumental to the achievement of victory. Indeed, Caesar seems to have been the first Roman commander to regard the siege as a concomitant part of general operations rather than as a separate discipline, and it is clear that he regarded passive blockade as a waste of resources. This readiness to commit his men to the pursuit of aggressive field entrenchment may have served him well, but Caesar was undoubtedly fortunate to have avoided serious defeats at both Corduba and Dyrrachium where his (more numerous) opponents were equally proficient in the rapid extemporization of field works. The well-publicized success of the tactics applied by Caesar no doubt resulted in their emulation by other Roman commanders, although the failure to appreciate the dynamic quality of the siege often led to these derivative actions leaving a more ponderous and laboured impression (particularly evident in the formulaic manner in which Octavian engaged in investment).

The importance of experienced soldiery to the prosecution of an effective siege is also hard to overstate. Caesar's veterans were not dismayed by the prospect of extending a lengthy encirclement or of raising a substantial assault ramp, having been habituated to such matters by long practice. However, where a formation was less familiar with the requisite techniques, or where the commander was uncertain of his tactical approach, there was a danger that the operation would become unduly protracted or, worse still, prove abortive. The Flavian campaign to suppress the Jewish Revolt can be seen as a case in point. After the disastrous rout of Cestius Gallus, Vespasian was properly circumspect in preparing for his advance against his first target at Iotapata. However, that he subsequently vacillated between a policy of pressing ahead with attempts at storming the wall and one involving more methodical preparations, suggests a lack of experience in pursuing operations against defenders capable of mounting aggressive sorties. Indeed, on more than one occasion it would seem that Vespasian lost the initiative and was forced to undertake reactive measures in the face of hostile pressure (such as a work of encirclement only reluctantly embarked upon). Inexperience can also be said to have marred Titus' attack on Jerusalem (for example, the failure to widen the breach in the Second wall and to fire the district beyond), but the frequently repeated process of ramp construction and the exposure to the daily routines of the siege camp certainly stood his men in good stead for the demands made upon them in the closing stages of the suppression campaign. Thus, although the Tenth legion had been severely embarrassed in the early days when its men had been caught by a sudden enemy sortie whilst dispersed in camp construction details on the Mount of Olives (clearly without the benefit of any covering screen), the competent manner in which this same unit subsequently undertook the investment of both Machaerus and Masada, suggests that the lessons of Jerusalem had been thoroughly absorbed.

Although these latter operations again emphasized the advantage of circumvallation as a preliminary to assault, it is only in exceptional circumstances that this tactic is repeated after the end of the first century AD. Whilst it may be tempting to view this omission as being symptomatic of a general decline in Roman siegecraft, the more likely explanation lies in the re-orientation of siege strategy towards the adoption of methods designed to effect a breach at the earliest possible opportunity. After all, the examples of Bethar and Cremna provide ample demonstration of the continuing capacity of the Roman army to mount operations where containment was regarded as an important objective. However, the failure to employ the Caesarian twin-track approach of containment and aggression in any systematic sense beyond the first century AD, must have resulted in a general, army-wide loss of expertise in the techniques of field fortification, and the serious cumulative consequences of this can be seen in the fourth-century anti-Sassanian campaigns of both Constantius and Julian. The former emperor, stuck before the walls of Bezabde, would appear to have run out of ideas after the Persians had stymied his assault by destroying his flimsy siege mounds, whilst the latter was obliged to issue orders over such a basic matter as the provision of adequate defences for his main base-camp following dangerous enemy sorties. However, both these commanders also employed sophisticated siege trains and instead of claiming that their campaigns lacked technical proficiency, it would be more accurate to suggest that two centuries of assault-first doctrines had left them ill-equipped to proceed with alternative approaches. Notwithstanding this identification of tactical shortcomings in these fourth-century campaigns, it would be wrong to assume that such weakness can be equated with a process of 'decline'. After all, even if Julian's Mesopotamian expedition had been handicapped by a limited methodological repertoire, this did little to arrest the triumphal progress made by his army in seizing a succession of defended centres along their route of march. Élan may well have been preferred to methodical probity, but as success in reductive operations must always be measured by the fall of the target, little criticism can be levelled at the strategic re-orientation that saw Roman offensive sieges become almost exclusively assault-driven affairs.

The role of archaeology in elucidating the details of the Roman siege system has been crucial. Even though many well-known sites were investigated in the late nineteenth and early twentieth centuries, this corpus of evidence has recently been supplemented by a small number of modern excavation/survey campaigns. The ambitious Franco-German undertaking at Alesia has demonstrated the value of applying modern area excavation techniques for the recovery of an impressive range of data concerning the elaboration of the Caesarian double investment as well as illustrating the important contribution that aerial photography can make. The role of remote sensing and geophysical techniques will no doubt prove influential in the future, particularly given the scale of many siege work elements, and unless the background geology proves unfavourable, it should be relatively simple to pick up the linear alignments and strong anomalies that might be expected from the features at most siege sites. In short, as we now have the technical capability to enhance our understanding both of the individual siege work elements and of their place within the overall siege system, it would be instructive to undertake a systematic programme to investigate a sample of sites selected over a broad chronological range. Hopefully the resulting data would provide insights not only into Roman siege methodology, but also furnish answers to specific questions concerning, for example, the capacity, purpose and requirements of ancient artillery, and address broader issues such as the degree to which technical skills and capabilities were disseminated throughout the Roman army.

NOTES

INTRODUCTION

1 Diod. Sic. XIII.2.1
2 Garlan 1974

I   THE LITERARY SOURCES

1 Caesar BC III.43-73
2 Florus II.13.39
3 Vell. Pat. II.68.3
4 Eutropius IX.23; Orosius VII.25.8
5 Val. Max. VII.6 ext 3
6 Val. Max. VII.6 ext 1
7 Polyb. XXIX.12.4-8
8 Caesar BG VII.52
9 idem VII.72-73 and see p.72-73; 78-79
10 idem VII.74
11 Josephus BJ III.162
12 Appian Pun.14.98
13 Diod. Sic. XX.95.1
14 Vel. Pat. II.47.1
15 Ogilvie 1965, 628
16 Livy V.10.7
17 Ogilvie 1965, 647
18 idem 205
19 Thucydides IV.29.2
20 Plutarch Marc.VI.5
21 Dio Cass. XL.34.2
22 Herodian VIII.5.5
23 SHA Maximini XXIII.4
24 Caesar BG VII.17-28
25 Orosius V.7.16; Florus I.34.15
26 Appian Hisp.15.97
27 Appian BC IV.10.80
28 Josephus BJ VII.320 et seq.
29 Dion. Hal. V.59.2
30 Livy I.43.3
31 idem I.53.4
32 Marsden 1969, 83
33 Livy V.5.2
34 idem V.5.5-6
35 see p.49-51
36 Livy V.1.9
37 Diod. Sic. XXIII.20
38 Livy XXI.61.8-11
39 Val. Max. VII.6.5
40 idem II.7.4
41 Zosimus I.70.4
42 idem I.54
43 Appian BC II.9.61
44 Florus I.45.25
45 Apoll. 137
46 Ambracia, Polyaen. VI.17; Babylon, Polyaen. VII.6.5; 6.8
47 Polyaen. III.10.5
48 For Cirrha, compare Frontinus Strateg. III.7
49 Polyaen. IV.18.1
50 idem VI.13
51 Lawrence 1979, 71
52 Philo IV.5
53 idem IV.6
54 idem IV.8
55 idem IV.52
56 idem IV.30
57 idem IV. 43-46; 50-56

58 *idem* IV.17-24

59 *idem* IV.10-11

60 Davies 2001, 60-62

61 Vitruvius x.16.12

62 *idem* x.16.Conclusion

63 Front. *Strateg.* III.Introduction

64 *idem* III.7

65 Onas. XL.1

66 *idem* XL.2

67 *idem* XLI.1

68 *idem* XLII.3-13

69 *idem* XLII.3

70 Vegetius IV.15

71 see p.114

72 Vegetius IV.24

73 *idem* IV.28

74 *loricula*

75 Vegetius IV.28

76 Comber 1997

77 Potter 1999

78 Rhegium, Polyb. 1.7.8-11; Syracuse, Livy
   XXV.29

79 Livy v.27

80 Val. Max. v.1.5

81 Cohen 1982

82 Astapa, Livy XXVIII.22-23; Abydus, Livy
   XXXI.17-18

83 Comber 1997, 52

84 Polyb. XII.28a.8-9

85 Crump 1975, 111

86 Amm. Marc. XXIV.4.23

87 *idem* XXIII.4.1-14

88 Josephus *Contr. Ap.* 1.55

89 e.g. Broshi 1982

90 Josephus *BJ* v.495-496

91 *idem* v.499-500

92 Broshi 1982, 380-381

93 Josephus *BJ* v.420

94 Broshi 1982, 381

95 Josephus *BJ* VII.306

96 Gill 1993, 570

97 in Schulten 1933a, 169

98 Josephus *BJ* VII.190

99 Strobel 1974b. 102-104

100 see p.78-79

101 Mitchell, Cormack *et al* 1995, 24

2   THE SIEGE IN THE CONTEXT OF ROMAN WARFARE

1 Dio Cassius LXVIII 31 (XIPH. 240 R ST.)

2 Austin and Rankov 1995

3 Livy XXXII. 16. 10

4 Josephus *BJ* v 539

5 Shatzman 1989, 470-473

6 Josephus *BJ* III. 141

7 Appian *Hisp.* 14.84

8 *idem* 14.84-85

9 *ibid*

10 *idem* 14.86

11 Livy *Per.* 57.2

12 Webster 1985, 173

13 Appian *Hisp.* 14.87-88

14 Livy XXXVI.22.7

15 *idem* XXXVI.34.9-10

16 Florus II.33.50

17 Caesar *BC* VII.13

18 *idem* VII.11

19 Dio Cass. LVI.12.3-5

20 Appian *BC* I.10.87-94

21 Caesar *BA* 79-80

22 Caesar *BH* 6-20

23 Caesar *BC* III.43-44

24 *idem* III.43

25 Livy XXIX.1.12-13

26 Josephus *BJ* II.528-540

27 SHA *Max.* XXII.4

28 Diod. Sic. XXI.5

29 *idem* XXI.3

30 Dio Cass. LXXVI.10.1

31 *idem* LXVIII.31.2

32 *idem* LXXVI.11-13.1

33 Caesar *BG* VII.17

34 *idem* VII.36

35 Josephus *BJ* IV.12

36 Sallust *BI* XXXVII.4; XXXVIII.1-2

37 Plutarch *Sert.*VIII.4-6

38 Appian *III.* 2.11

39 Diod. Sic. XXXVI.5

40 Amm. Marc. XVII.2.2-3

41 Diod. Sic. XXIII.18.4

42 Livy XXXVIII.3.11

43 Amm. Marc. XX.11.23
44 Roth 1995, 90
45 Roth 1995
46 Memnon 47-52
47 Appian *Pun.* 3.16

48 Livy XXIV.34.4-7
49 Livy XXVII.25.11
50 Amm. Marc. XXVI.8.9
51 Dio Cass. XLIX.37.5
52 Amm. Marc. XXI.12.9

3   PREPARATORY WORKS

1 Dio Cassius LXVIII.31 (Xiph. 240 R St.)
2 Livy XXXVIII.3.11
3 Xanthus, Appian *BC* IV.10.76; Ursao, Caesar *BH* 41
4 Zosimus III.13.3
5 Sallust *BI LXXV-LXXVI*
6 Livy XXV.20.3
7 Caesar *BG* VII.11
8 *idem* VII.18-19
9 *idem* VII.36
10 see p.56
11 Josephus *BJ* III.142
12 Dio Cass. LXVIII.31.2
13 Onas. X.16
14 Livy XXXIV38.1
15 *idem* XXXVI.22.4
16 Amm. Marc. XXIV.4.3
17 Livy XXXVIII.4.4
18 Caesar *BG* VII.17
19 Appian *Pun.* 14.99
20 Harmand 1967, 119-126
21 Bénard 1987, 38-39
22 Josephus *BJ* V.259-260
23 Dio Cass. XIX (Zon. 9.18)
24 Josephus *BJ* V.70
25 e.g., Vegetius 1.21-25
26 Appian *Hisp.* 14.86

27 Livy *Per.* 57.2
28 Schulten 1933b, 111-112
29 Caesar *BC* I.16
30 Josephus *BJ* V.133-134
31 Amm. Marc. XXIV4.6
32 Appian *Hisp.*12.69
33 Josephus *BJ* V.106
34 Polyb. XXI.26.4
35 Appian *Hisp.*15.90
36 Schulten 1933b, 95-96
37 Caesar *BG* VII.72
38 Reddé and von Schnurbein 2001, 388-390
39 Bénard 1987, 39
40 Le Gall 1989, 304-305. Although the feature may be associated with the defences of Vercingetorix's camp *per* Caesar *BG* VII.69.
41 Le Gall 1976, 64
42 Caesar *BG* VII.72
43 Val. Max. VII.6.5
44 Davies 2001b
45 Josephus *BJ* V.107-8; 130-134
46 *idem* IV.13-17
47 *idem* IV.10; Bar-Kochva 1976, 69-70
48 Livy XXXVI.22.11
49 Wilson 1974
50 SHA *Aur.* XXVIII.2
51 Amm. Marc. XXIII.3.9

4   BLOCKADE CAMPS

1 Dion. Hal. III.40.1
2 *idem* III.50.4
3 Livy I.57.4
4 Livy II.33.6-8
5 Livy V.2.1
6 Palaeopolis, Livy VIII.23.10; 25.5-8; Saticula, Livy IX.21.2-6; Bovianum, Livy IX.28.1-3
7 see p.49-50
8 see p.51

9 see p.51-52
10 Polyb. 1.48.10
11 Livy XXIV.39.13
12 Livy XXVI.42.6; Polyb.X.9.7
13 see p.53
14 Caesar *BG* VII.17
15 Yadin 1971
16 Yadin 1963b, 14
17 Vegetius 1.21

18 Welfare and Swan 1995
19 Milner 1993, 22 note 3.
20 Amm. Marc. XX.11.6
21 *idem* XXIV.4.6
22 *idem* XXIV.5.12
23 e. g. Salvatore 1996
24 Livy V.1.9
25 see p.14
26 Livy V.2.1
27 'supertas munitiones' Livy V.8.10
28 'maiora castra' Livy V.8.12.
29 Livy V.12.4
30 'circa munimenta' Livy V.13.9
31 Livy IX.25.5
32 Livy IX.22.2
33 Polyb. I.17.8
34 *idem* I.18.3-4
35 *idem* I.42.8
36 *idem* I.48.9
37 Livy XXV.25.8
38 Appian *Pun.* 14.100
39 *idem* 17.113
40 *idem* 18.119
41 *idem* 18.120

42 see p.129-131
43 Appian *Pun.* 18.125
44 Josephus *AJ* XIV.86-90; *BJ* I.164-168
45 Meshel 1984
46 Shatzman 1991, 69-71
47 Caesar *BG* VII.36
48 *ibid*
49 Napoleon III 1866, 270-271, n.3
50 Caesar *BG* VII.40
51 Jobey 1978, 81
52 RCAHMS 1997, 181
53 Christison and Barbour 1899, 219-220; 235-236
54 Yadin 1963b, 13
55 Appian *Hisp.* 13.78
56 Sallust *BI* LRXI.1
57 Caesar *BC* III.9
58 Caesar *BA* 80
59 Caesar *BH* 6
60 Amm. Marc. XX.11.6
61 *idem* XXIV.4.6
62 *idem* XXIV.5.12

5 CIRCUMVALLATION

1 Velitrae, Dion. Hal. III.41.5; Fidenae, Dion. Hal. V.58.2
2 at Mt Algidus (458 BC), Livy III.28.2-8 and Ardea (443 BC), Livy IV.9.13-14
3 See p.14
4 Livy VI.8.9
5 See p.51-52 for discussion
6 Livy XXV.22.16
7 Livy XXVIII.3.5
8 Livy XXXVIII.4.6
9 Appian *Hisp.*12.69
10 See p.26
11 See p.70
12 Praeneste, Appian *BC* I.10.88; Perusia, Appian *BC* V.4.33
13 Sallust *BI* LXXV-LXXVI
14 Aduatuci, Caesar *BG* II.30; Ategua, Caesar *BH* 6; Dio Cass. XLIII.33

16 see p.72-73; 78-79
17 Appian *III.* 4.23
18 Florus II.33.50; Orosius VI.21.5
19 see p.111-112
20 Davies 2001, Appendix A, 341-343
21 Dio Cass. LXXV.10-13; Herodian III.6.9
22 Davies 2002
23 Davies 2000
24 Vegetius IV.28
25 Vegetius I.21
26 e.g. at Promona (34 BC), Appian *III.* 5.26
27 Zertal 1995, 90
28 Velitrae and Fidenae, above note 1; Antium, Dion. Hal. X.21.5
29 Polyb. I.18.3-4
30 Polyb.I.19.13
31 Polyb. I.48.10

32 Athens, Appian *Mith.* 6.38; Pitane, Appian
   Mith. 8.52; Tigranocerta, Appian *Mith.* 12.84;
   Segesta, Appian *III.* 4.23; Mt Medullus, Florus
   II.33.50; Orosius VI.21.5
33 Diod. Sic. XXIII.18.4
34 Livy IV.22.3
35 Anxur, Livy V.12.6; Satricum, Livy VI.8.9
36 Livy XXVIII.3.5
37 Livy XXV.22.16
38 Appian *Hann.* 6.37
39 Appian *Hisp.* 15.90
40 Schulten 1914-1931, Vol.III, 82-83
41 Appian *Hisp.* 15.92
42 Plutarch *Crassus* X.5
43 Appian *BC* V.4.33
44 Appian *BC* V.4.36
45 Appian *BC* V.4.38
46 Caesar *BG* VII.74
47 Reddé and von Schnurbein 2001
48 *idem* 312-323
49 *idem* 323-327
50 *idem* 333-342
51 Richmond and St Joseph 1982
52 Reddé and von Schnurbein 2001, 225
53 Zertal 1995, 77
54 Mitchell, Cormack *et al* 1995, 201
55 Strobel 1974b, 120-122
56 Strobel 1974a, 155
57 Schulten 1933a, 93
58 *idem 182*
59 see Davies 2000
60 Cremna, Mitchell, Cormack *et al* 1995, 201;
   Narbata, Zertal 1995, 77; Masada, Schulten
   1933a, 93
61 Caesar *BG* VII.72
62 Appian *Hisp.* 15.90
63 Davies 2002
64 Andrae 1912, 20-21
65 Caesar *BG* VII.73
66 Reddé and von Schnurbein 2001, 359-366
67 *idem* 457
68 *idem* 436-440
69 *idem* 327-333
70 *idem* 359-366
71 *idem* 201-205; 454-460
72 Reddé and von Schnurbein 2001, 350-358
73 Sil.Ital. Pun XIII.105
74 Appian *Pun.* 18.120
75 Appian *Hisp.* 15.90
76 Caesar *BG* VII.72
77 Appian *BC* V.4.33
78 Caesar *BH* 19
79 Caesar *BH* 13
80 Reddé, von Schnurbein *et al* 1995, 99;
   Reddé and von Schnurbein 2001, 342-349
81 Reddé, von Schnurbein *et al* 1995, 103
82 Reddé and von Schnurbein 2001, 385
83 *idem* 221
84 Schulten 1914-1931 Vol.III, 85
85 *idem* 218-220; Schulten 1933b, 121
86 Hawkes 1929a, 202; Schulten 1933a,
   93; Richmond 1962, 153; Davies 2001
   Appendix A, 379-380
87 Richmond 1962, 154
88 Strobel 1974a, 148
89 *contra* Strobel 1974b, 117
90 Davies 2000, 152
91 *idem* 157
92 Campbell 1984
93 Amm. Marc. XXIII.4.5
94 Davies 2001 Appendix A, 351
95 Cichorius Plate LXVI, Cast 166
96 Lepper and Frere 1988, 106
97 Appian *Hann.* 6.37
98 Caesar *BC* I.18
99 Appian *Hisp.* 15.90
100 Josephus *BJ* V.106
101 Appian *Hisp.*15.97
102 Schulten 1914-1931 Vol III
103 Schulten 1933a, 105; 137
104 Agrigentum, Polyb.I.18.2; Corfinium,
   Caesar *BC* I.18; Numantia, Appian *Hisp.* 15.90
105 Kennedy and Riley 1990, 103
106 The identification of an assault ramp by
   Yadin 1971, 192-193 has been called into
   doubt (Ussishkin 1993, 95) with good
   reason
107 Schulten 1933a, 182
108 *idem* 140; 145
109 suggested by Richmond 1962, 152
110 Schulten 1933a, 146-155
111 Davies 2001 Appendix A, 380
112 Strobel 1974a; Davies 2001 Appendix A,
   372-373
113 Strobel 1974a, 146
114 *idem* 147

115 *idem* 157
116 see p.29
117 Caesar BC III.63
118 Dodge 1995, 516
119 Appian BC II.9.61; Plutarch *Crassus* X.5
120 Appian *Hisp.* 15.90
121 Appian BC V.4.33
122 Josephus *BJ* V.508
123 Reddé 1999, 123
124 as argued for Narbata, Machaerus and Bethar: Zertal 1995, 90

125 *idem* 80
126 Appian *Hann.* 6.37
127 *contra* Sil. Ital. XIII.105–109
128 Appian BC I.10.88
129 Mitchell, Cormack *et al* 1995, 203
130 Roth 1995, 100
131 Richmond 1962, 153
132 Livy XXXIV.39–40
133 Caesar BG VII.11
134 Josephus *BJ* V.502–509
135 *idem* 509

6 ASSAULT RAMPS AND SIEGE MOUNDS

1 For early Hittite usage see Yadin 1963a, 70–71
2 For Assyrian usage at Lachish see Ussishkin 1978; 1983; 1990; 1996. For Persian usage at Palaepaphos see Maier 1967–9; 1973)
3 Davies 2001, 60–62
4 Dionysius Hal. v.59.2
5 Livy V.7.2–3
6 Livy VI.8.9
7 At Panormus, rams were deployed "after making the other necessary preparations" (Polyb. 1.38.8) – presumably the filling in of the town ditch; at Lipara the defenders succeeded in burning the Roman *agger* (Val. Max. II.7.4); at Lilybaeum, the Carthaginians attempted to undermine the Roman ramp but were unable to compete with the greater labour resources of the Romans (who were presumably able to keep pace with any resulting subsidence), Dio Cass. XII (Zon. 8.15)
8 Livy VIII.16.8
9 *Pun.* XIII.109
10 Livy XXXII.17.17
11 Appian *Mith.* 5.36
12 Caesar BG III.21
13 Caesar BG VII.24
14 Josephus *BJ* I.145–147
15 Appian *Pun.* 14.98
16 Amm. Marc. XXIV.2.11
17 Caesar BG VIII.41
18 Caesar BC II.1; II.15
19 For Cremna see below p.108; Bezabde, Amm Marc. XX.11.20

20 For Lachish and Palaepaphos see note 2 above; for Old Smyrna see Nicholls 1958-9, 88–91; Cook 1958-9, 24
21 Peter Connolly *pers comm*
22 Segment II–IV of the reliefs (Ussishkin 1982, Figs.159 & 160), *contra* the suggestion (Eph'al 1984, 67) that they were intended to cause a breach.
23 Maier 1967, 40; Wilson 1974
24 Livy XXXVI.22.7–11;23.2
25 Appian BC IV.8.60
26 Appian *Mith.* 5.30
27 Appian BC IV.10.76
28 Ussishkin 1990, 64
29 Mitchell, Cormack *et al* 1995, 198, Fig 53
30 Caesar BC II.2
31 Caesar BG VII.24
32 For Noviodunum, Caesar BG II.12; for the Aduatuci, Caesar BG II.30–31
33 Josephus *BJ* V.302
34 Josephus *BJ* V.466
35 Josephus *BJ* VI.5
36 Josephus *BJ* VI.149
37 Josephus *BJ* VI.392
38 Appian BC IV.8.60
39 Ussishkin 1990, 60; 64
40 Maier 1967, 39; 1973, Fig 1
41 Strobel 1974a, 156
42 Gill 1993, 570; Lammerer 1933, 169
43 Comte du Mesnil 1939, 64
44 Caesar BC II.1
45 Stoffel 1887, 82

46 Caesar *BG* VIII.41

47 Mitchell, Cormack *et al* 1995, 180

48 Napoleon III 1866, pl. 20; Comte du Mesnil 1939; Wimmel 1974

49 Livy XXXII.17.17

50 Ussishkin 1990, 64

51 Ussishkin 1996, 18

52 Ussishkin 1990, 67-9

53 see Nicholls 1958-9, 88-91; 128, note 112; Fig 27

54 Roth 1995, 102

55 Mitchell, Cormack *et al* 1995, 180

56 *ibid*

57 Peter Connolly *pers comm*

58 Cichorius Plate LXXV, Cat 196

59 Thucydides II.75.2

60 Sil. Ital. *Pun.* XIII.109

61 Lucan III.396-398

62 *idem* 455

63 Amm. Marc. XX.11.23

64 Josephus *BJ* V.466-480

65 Peter Connolly *pers comm*

66 Gill 1993, 569

67 Caesar *BG* VII.22

68 Josephus *BJ* VII.307

69 cf. his exaggeration of the height of the ramp on p.22

70 Davies 2000

71 Caesar *BC* II.2 – the defenders possessed engines capable of projecting spiked beams, 12ft long through four layers of hurdles

72 Amm. Marc. XIX.8.2-3

73 Peter Connolly *pers comm*

74 Thucydides II.77.3

75 Josephus *BJ* V.275

76 Josephus *BJ* III.267-272

77 Appian *III.* 4.20

78 Caesar *BG* VII.24

7   MINES

1 e.g. Persian use of mines at Barca and Chalcedon late in the 6th century BC, Aen. Tact. XXXVII.6-7; Polyaenus VII.11.5; Greek use of mines at 'Egyptian' Larisa, 399 BC, Xenophon III.1.7, Gaza, 332 BC, Curtius IX.8.13-14 and Lilybaeum, 276 BC, Livy XXXVI.25.4

2 Fidenae, Dion. Hal. III.40.1, *idem* V.59.2 and Livy IV.22.5; Veii, Livy V.19.10-11

3 *contra* Lammert 1932, 1774

4 as Polybius states for Ambracia, XXI.28.3

5 Livy XXXVIII.7.6; Polyb. XXI.28

6 the Piraeus, Appian *Mith.* 5.36; Avaricum, Caesar *BG* VII.22

7 the Piraeus, Appian *Mith.* 5.36; the Sotiates, Caesar *BG* III.21

8 Caesar *BG* VIII.41

9 Ambracia, Polyaenus VI.17; Themiscyra, Appian *Mith.* 11.78

10 Josephus *BJ* V.491-501

11 Vegetius IV.24

12 Amm. Marc. XXIV.4.12; XXIV.4.21

13 Curtius IV.6.8

14 Napoleon III 1866, 346

15 Livy XXXVI.25.4

16 Caesar *BG* VIII.41; VIII.43

17 Napoleon III 1866, 345-346 and see Labrousse 1966, 567 n.5

18 Maier 1967, 41

19 Maier 1973, 189

20 Maier 1967, 41

21 *ibid*

22 Comte du Mesnil 1936

23 *idem* 188

24 *idem* 200

25 *ibid*

26 *idem* 201

27 *idem* 203

28 *ibid*

29 *idem* 190

30 driving fire-hardened stakes into the ground at Avaricum, Caesar *BG* VII.22; excavating a deep fosse to deny Demetrius' miners at Rhodes, Diod. Sic. XX.94.2

31 M. Hassall *pers comm. contra* de Mély 1931

32 Livy IV.22.5

33 *idem* V.21.4

34 Polyb. XXI.28.3

35 Polyaenus VII.11.5

36 e.g. Ancus Marcius' alleged tunnel at Fidenae in the 620s BC was started within the shelter of his camp. Dion. Hal. III.40.1

37 Comte du Mesnil 1936, 188

38 Livy v.19.10-11

39 Polyb. XXI.28.5

40 Caesar *BG* III.21

41 Zos. III.22.1

42 "*delectis militibus*" Livy v.21.10

43 Amm. Marc. XXIV.4.23; Zos. III.22.4

8 MISCELLANEOUS ENGINEERING WORKS

1 e.g. widening/strengthening the isthmus at both Carthage, 149 BC and at Laodicea, 43 BC

2 Dio Cass. XII (Zon. 8.16)

3 Caesar *BG* III.12

4 Polyb. I.47.4

5 Diod. Sic. XXIV.3-5

6 Appian *Pun.* 18.124

7 Caesar *BC* I.25-28

8 Pan. Lat. VIII.6.2

9 Herodian VII.12.4

10 Front. *Strat.* III.7.1

11 Caesar *BC* III.49

12 Plut. *Pomp.* XXXII.4

13 Dio Cass. XLVI.36

14 Front. *Strat.* III.14.3

15 Appian *Hisp.* 15.91

16 Plut. *Brut.* XXX.4

17 Amm. Marc. XX.11.11

18 Livy XXIX.35.8

19 Gytheum, Livy XXXIV.29.5; Ambracia, Livy XXXVIII.5.1

20 Schulten 1934a, 162

21 Richmond 1962, 154

22 Roth 1995, 94

23 For further discussion see Davies 2001, Appendix A, 383-384

24 Reddé and von Schnurbein 2001, 425-430

25 Caesar *BC* II.8

26 *idem* II.9

27 *idem* II.10

28 *idem* II.15

GLOSSARY

ASSAULT RAMP
Structure raised to parallel the height of a defensive work enabling the passage of storming parties and the mounting of engines capable of effecting a breach (cf. SIEGE MOUND).

BALLISTARIUM(A)
Prepared, raised platform, usually rectangular/sub-rectangular in shape, allowing the mounting of heavy artillery.

BERM
Clear space left between the rampart front and the inner lip of any ditch fronting it, preventing the slippage of the former into the latter; or the interval between two ditches in a multiple-ditch system.

BLOCKADE CAMP
Specific class of siege work designed as a base from which the besieger might act to interdict supplies or reinforcements sent to a defended position or to prevent sorties or foraging efforts mounted from the same. May take several forms from a single large encampment (with or without branching spurs) to a series of camps linked by entrenchment (the latter to be distinguished from a line of circumvallation by the incomplete nature of the investment and the fact that further active measures may be required to maintain the blockade).

CHEMIN DES RONDES
Patrol walk along the top of a wall with a parapet for cover.

CHEVAL (AUX)-DE-FRISE
Obstacle field comprising sharpened stakes or jagged stones placed in advance of the outer counterscarp to delay/disrupt attackers.

CIPPUS (I)
Series of prepared branches fastened together at the base and set in a trench, the sharpened ends projecting above the ground surface to form a continuous entanglement.

CIRCUMVALLATION
In a generic (and imprecise) sense, any form of encircling work designed to complete an investment. In those siege systems that deploy two distinct encircling lines however, the circumvallation forms that line facing outwards to confront any external threat (cf. CONTRAVALLATION).

CLAVICULA
Device to counter direct attacks on an entrance or gateway achieved by extending the rampart and any ditch on one side in a sharp, stubby arc to form a defended passageway (cf. TITULUM).

CONTRAVALLATION
In the course of this book, this term is *only* used where there are two separate lines of investment, in which case it refers to the inner line (including both rampart and any forward installations) facing the defended position (cf. CIRCUMVALLATION).

COUNTERSCARP
Outer side of a ditch.

ENCEINTE
Main line of any defensive perimeter.

ENFILADE FIRE
Artillery or missile fire directed from a flanking position to sweep a line of works in a longitudinal manner

LILIUM (A)
Mantrap deployed in front of a defensive line to disrupt the momentum of an attack comprising an inward sloping pit with a sharpened stake bedded into the base and concealed by means of brushwood etc.

POINT D'APPUI
The main point of attack.

REDUIT
A citadel or strongpoint of last resort.

SIEGE MOUND
Structure raised to parallel or overtop the height of a defensive work allowing oversight of the defenders and the advantageous emplacement of artillery. Although primarily designed to fulfil a suppressive role, the siege mound (depending upon its siting) could be adapted to act as an ASSAULT RAMP.

SIEGE SYSTEM
The general tactical deployment adopted by a besieger to achieve the reduction of a defended position comprising the totality of various disparate siege work elements.

SIEGE WORK
Any structure or feature constructed by an assailant for the purpose of prosecuting operations (directly or indirectly) against a defended position.

STADE
Greek unit of measurement equivalent to approximately 600ft.

STIMULUS (I)
Short, buried stake or log with protruding iron spike(s) deployed as an obstacle in advance of or between, lines of defence.

TESTUDO
Close-order infantry formation involving the linkage of overlapping shields to provide cover against enemy missile fire or, alternatively, a mobile covered gallery or penthouse advanced against the enemy wall.

TITULUM (I)
Short, displaced rampart and ditch placed in advance of an entrance or gateway to disrupt the momentum of any attack (cf. *CLAVICULA*).

BIBLIOGRAPHY

A. PRIMARY SOURCES

AENEAS TACTICUS
How to survive under 1990. Whitehead, D. (trans.). Oxford, Clarendon Press.
siege

AMMIANUS MARCELLINUS
Res Gestae 1935–1939. Rolfe, J.C. (trans.). Loeb Classical Library.

APOLLODORUS OF DAMASCUS
Poliorcetica 1693. Poliorcetica excerpta. In: *Veteres Mathematici*. 13–48. Paris.
1908. Schneider, R. (trans.). reichische Poliorketiker.
Abhandlungen der Königlichen Gesellschaft der Wissenschaften zu Göttingen. Neue Folge, **X**, 1-65.

APPIAN
Roman History 1912–1913. White, H. (trans.). Loeb Classical Library.

CAESAR
Bellum Civile 1914. Page, T.E. (trans.). Loeb Classical Library.

De Bello Africo
De Bello Alexandrino } 1988. Way, A.G. (trans.). Loeb Classical Library.
De Bello Hispaniensi

De Bello Gallico 1980. Wiseman, A. & Wiseman, P. (trans.). *The Battle for Gaul*. London, BCA.
1994. Edwards, H.J. (trans.). Loeb Classical Library.

CICERO
Epistulae ad Atticum 1952–1953. Winstedt, E.O. (trans.). Loeb Classical Library.
Epistulae ad Familiares 1927–1929. Williams, W.G. (trans.). Loeb Classical Library.

CURTIUS
Historiarum Alexandri   1946. Rolfe, J.C. (trans.). Loeb Classical Library.
Magni

DIO CASSIUS
Roman History   1914-1927. Cary, E. (trans.). Loeb Classical Library.

DIODORUS SICULUS
The Library of History   1933-1967. Oldfather, C.H. (trans.). Books I-XV.19. Sherman,
          C.L. (trans.). Books XV.20-XVI.65. Loeb Classical Library.

DIONYSIUS OF HALICARNASSUS
Roman Antiquities   1937-1950. Cary, E. (trans.). Loeb Classical Library.

EUTROPIUS
Breviarium   1993. Bird, H.W. (trans.). Liverpool University Press.

FLORUS
Epitome   1984. Forster, E.S. (trans.). Loeb Classical Library.

FRONTINUS
Strategemata   1925. Bennett, C.E. (trans.). Loeb Classical Library.

HERODIAN
History   1969-1970. Whittaker, C.R. (trans.). Loeb Classical Library.

JOSEPHUS
Bellum Judaicum   1927-1928. Thackeray, H. St. J. (trans.). Loeb Classical Library.
Jewish Antiquities   1986. Marcus, R. (trans.). Vol. VII. Loeb Classical Library.

LIVY
Ab Urbe Condita   1919-1929. Foster, B.O. (trans.). Books I-IX.
          1940-1949. Moore, F.G. (trans.) Books X-XXX.
          1935-1936. Sage, E.T. (trans.). Books XXXI-XXXIX.
          1938-1951. Schlesinger, A.C. (trans.). Books XL-XLV. Loeb
          Classical Library.
Periochae   1984. Jal, P. (trans.). Paris, Collections des Universités de France.

LUCAN
De Bello Civili   1962. Duff, J.D. (trans.). Loeb Classical Library.

MEMNON

1950. Jacoby, F. (trans.). *Die Fragmente der Griechischen Historiker.* 36.434, 336-368. Leiden, Brill.

ONASANDER

The General   1986. The Illinois Greek Club (trans.). Loeb Classical Library.

OROSIUS

Historiarum Adversus   1990-1991. Arnaud-Lindet, M-P. (trans.). Paris, Collections des
Paganos   Universités de France.

PANEGYRICI LATINI

1994. Nixon, C.E.V. & Rodgers, B.S. (trans.). Berkeley, University of California Press.

PHILO OF BYZANTIUM

Poliorketika   1974. Garlan, Y. (trans.). *Recherches de Poliorcétique Grecque,* 291–327.
               1979. Lawrence, A.W. (trans.). *Greek Aims in Fortification,* 73–107.

PLUTARCH

Lives   1914-1926. Perrin, B. (trans.). Loeb Classical Library.

POLYAENUS

Stratagems of War   1994. Krentz, P. & Wheeler, E.L. (trans.). Chicago, Ares
               Publishers Inc.

POLYBIUS

The Histories   1922-1927. Paton, W.R. (trans.). Loeb Classical Library.

SALLUST

Historiae   1992-1994. McGushin, P. (trans.). Oxford, Clarendon Press.

SCRIPTORES HISTORIAE AUGUSTAE

1922-1932. Magie, D. (trans.). Loeb Classical Library.

SILIUS ITALICUS

Punica   1961. Duff, J.D. (trans.). Loeb Classical Library.

THUCYDIDES

History of the   1951-1953. Smith, C.F. (trans.). Loeb Classical Library.
Peloponnesian War

VALERIUS MAXIMUS

Factorum et Dictorum   1971. Faranda, R. (trans.). Turin, Classici Latini.

Memorabilium   1995-1997. Combès, R. (trans.). Books I-VI. Paris, Les Belles
                  Lettres.

VEGETIUS

Epitoma Rei Militaris   1993. Milner, N.P. (trans.). Liverpool University Press.

VELLEIUS PATERCULUS

Historiae Romanae   1979. Shipley, F.W. (trans.). Loeb Classical Library.

VITRUVIUS

De Architectura   1934. Granger, F. (trans.). Loeb Classical Library.

XENOPHON

Hellenica   1985. Brownson, C.L. (trans.). Loeb Classical Library.

ZOSIMUS

Nea Historia   1990. Ridley, R.T. (trans.). Canberra, Australian Association for
                  Byzantine Studies.

B. SECONDARY SOURCES

Aharoni, Y. 1961. The Caves of Nahal Hever. '*Atiqot* **III**, 148-162.

Andrae, W. 1908. Nach Aufnahmen von Mitgliedern der Assur-Expedition der Deutschen Orient-Gesellschaft. Vol.I. Allgemeine Beschreibung der Ruinen. *Wissenschaftliche Veröffentlichung der Deutschen Orient-Gesellschaft (WVDOG)* **9**. Leipzig.

Andrae, W. 1912. Nach Aufnahmen von Mitgliedern der Assur-Expedition der Deutschen Orient-Gesellschaft. Vol.II. Einzelbeschreibung der Ruinen. *WVDOG* **21**. Leipzig.

Austin, N.J.E. & Rankov, N.B. 1995. *Exploratio: Military and Political Intelligence in the Roman world*. Routledge, London.

Bahat, D. 1990. *The Illustrated Atlas of Jerusalem*. Simon & Schuster, New York.

Bar-Kochva, B. 1976. Gamla in Gaulanitis. *Zeitschrift des deutschen Palästina-Vereins*. **92**, 54-71.

Bénard, J. 1987. César devant Alesia: les témoins sont dans le sol. *Revue Historiques des Armées*. **2**, 29-55.

Broshi, M. 1982. The Credibility of Josephus. *Journal of Jewish Studies*. **33**, 379-384.

Campbell, D.B. 1984. *Ballistaria* in first to mid-third century Britain: a reappraisal. *Britannia*. **15**, 75-84.

Christison D. & Barbour, J. 1899. Account of the Excavation of the Camps and Earthworks at Birrenswark Hill, in Annandale, Undertaken by the Society in 1898. *Proceedings of the Society of Antiquaries of Scotland*. **33**, 198-249.

Cohen, S.J.D. 1982. Masada: Literary Tradition, Archaeological Remains, and the

Credibility of Josephus. *Journal of Jewish Studies*. **33**, 385-405.

Comber, M. 1997. Re-reading the Roman Historians. In: Bentley, M. (ed.) *Companion to Historiography*. 43-56. Routledge, London.

Comte du Mesnil du Buisson, R. 1936. The Persian Mines. In: Rostovtzeff, M.I., Bellinger, A.R., Hopkins, C. & Welles, C.B. (eds) *Excavations at Dura-Europos, Sixth Season 1932-33*, 188-205. Yale University Press.

Comte du Mesnil du Buisson, R. 1939. Du siège d'Avaricum a celui de Doura-Europos. *Revue Archéologique VI Sér.* **13**, 60-72.

Cook, J.M. 1958-1959. Old Smyrna, 1948-1951. *The Annual of the British School at Athens*. **53-54**, 1-34.

Crump, G.A. 1975. Ammianus Marcellinus as a Military Historian. *Historia*. Einzelschriften Heft **27**. Frank Steiner Verlag, Wiesbaden.

Davies, G. 2000. Cremna in Pisidia: a re-appraisal of the siege works. *Anatolian Studies*, **50**, 151-158.

Davies, G. 2001. *Roman Offensive Siege Works*. Unpublished PhD Thesis, Institute of Archaeology, UCL.

Davies, G. 2001b. Siege works, psychology and symbolism. In Davies, G., Gardener, A. & Lockyear, K. (eds) *Proceedings of the Tenth Annual Theoretical Archaeology Conference, London 2000*. 69-79. Oxbow, Oxford.

Davies, G. 2002. The Circumvallation at Hatra. In Freeman, P. *et al* (eds) *Proceedings of the 18th International Congress of Roman Frontier Studies*, **1**, 281-286. BAR Int. Series 1084(1).

Dodge, T.A. 1995 (reprint). *Caesar*. Greenhill Books, London.

Eph'al, I. 1984. The Assyrian Siege Ramp at Lachish: Military and Lexical Aspects. *Tel Aviv*. **11**, 60-70.

Garlan, Y. 1974. *Recherches de Poliorcétique Grecque*. Bibliothèque des Écoles Françaises d' Athènes et de Rome. Fasc. **223**.

Gill, D. 1993. A natural spur at Masada. *Nature*. **364**, 569-570.

Harmand, J. 1967. *Une Campagne Césarienne, Alésia*. A. & J. Picard, Paris.

Hawkes, C.F.C. 1929a. The Roman Siege of Masada. *Antiquity*. **3**, 195-213.

Hawkes, C.F.C. 1929b. Review of 'Numantia: die Ergebnisse der Ausgrabungen, 1905-1912'. *Journal of Roman Studies*. **19**, 99-102.

Jobey, G. 1978. Burnswark Hill, Dumfriesshire. *Transactions of the Dumfriesshire and Galloway Natural History and Antiquarian Society*. **53**, 57-104.

Johnson, A. 1983. *Roman Forts*. Adam & Charles Black, London.

Johnson, S. 1983. *Late Roman Fortifications*. Batsford, London.

Kennedy, D. & Riley, D. 1990. *Rome's Desert Frontier from the Air*. Batsford, London.

Lammerer, von H.C. 1933. Der Angriffsdamm. In: Schulten 1933a *infra*, 167-171.

Lawrence, A.W. 1979. *Greek Aims in Fortification*. Oxford University Press, Oxford.

Le Gall, J. 1976. Le Siège d' Alésia. *Archéologia*. **100**, 56-65.

Le Gall, J. 1989. *Fouilles d' Alise Ste. Reine, 1861-1865*. Memoires de l'Académie des Inscriptions et Belles-Lettres. 2 Vols. Paillert, Paris.

Lepper, F. & Frere, S. 1988. *Trajan's Column*. Alan Sutton, Gloucester.

Maier, F.G. 1967. Excavations at Kouklia (Palaepaphos), Site A. Preliminary report. *Report of the Department of Antiquities, Cyprus, 1967.* 30-49.

Maier, F.G. 1968. Excavations at Kouklia (Palaepaphos). Second preliminary report. *Report of the Department of the Antiquities, Cyprus, 1968.* 86-93.

Maier, F.G. 1969. Excavations at Kouklia (Palaepaphos). Third preliminary report. *Report of the Department of Antiquities, Cyprus, 1969.* 33-42.

Maier, F.G. 1973. Excavations at Kouklia (Palaepaphos). Sixth preliminary report. *Report of the Department of Antiquities, Cyprus, 1973.* 186-198.

Marsden, E.W. 1969. *Greek and Roman Artillery: Historical Development.* Clarendon, Oxford.

Marsden, E.W. 1971. *Greek and Roman Artillery: Technical Treatises.* Clarendon, Oxford.

Mély de, F. 1931. Les trompettes de Jéricho et la Grêle d'Aérolithes de Gabaon. *Revue Archéologique.* **33**, 111-116.

Meshel, Z. 1984. The Fortification System during the Hasmonaean Period. In: Schiller, E. (ed.) *Zev Vilnay's Jubilee Volume-Part 1.* 254-258. Aris Publishing, Jerusalem (Hebrew).

Milner, N.P. 1993. *Vegetius: Epitome of Military Science.* Liverpool University Press.

Mitchell, S., Cormack, S., Fursdon, R., Owens, E. & Öztürk, J. 1995. *Cremna in Pisidia: An Ancient City in Peace and War.* Duckworth and The Classical Press of Wales, London.

Napoleon III. 1866. *Histoire de Jules César. Tome II. Guerre des Gaules.* H.Plon, Paris.

Nicholls, R.V. 1958-1959. Old Smyrna : The Iron Age Fortifications, Etc. *The Annual of the British School at Athens.* **53-54**, 35-137.

Ogilvie, R.M. 1965. *A Commentary on Livy.* Clarendon Press, Oxford.

Potter, D.S. 1999. *Literary Texts and the Roman Historian.* Routledge, London.

Reddé, M. 1999. César Ante Alesia. In: Almagro-Gorbea, M., Blázquez Martínez, J.M., Reddé, M., Echegaray, J.G., Sádaba, J.L.R. & Peralta Labrador, E. *Las Guerras Cántabras.* 119-144. Fundación Marcelino Botín, Santander.

Reddé, M., von Schnurbein, S., Barral, P., Bénard, J., Brouquier-Reddé, V., Goguey, R., Joly, M., Köhler, H-J. & Petit, C. 1995. Fouilles et recherches nouvelles sur les travaux de César devant Alésia (1991-1994). *Bericht der Römisch-Germanischen Kommission.* **76**, 73-158.

Reddé, M. & von Schnurbein, S. *et al* (eds.) 2001. *Alésia. Fouilles et recherches Franco-Allemandes sur les travaux militaries Romains autour du Mont-Auxois (1991-1997). Vol. 1. Les Fouilles.* Mémoires de l'Académie des Inscriptions et Belles-Lettres **12**. Diffusion de Boccard, Paris.

Richmond, I.A. 1962. The Roman Siege-Works of Masada. *Journal of Roman Studies.* **52**, 142-155.

Richmond, I.A. & St Joseph, J.K.S. 1982. Excavations at Woden Law, 1950. *Proceedings of the Society of Antiquaries of Scotland.* **112**, 277-284.

Roth, J. 1995. The Length of the Siege of Masada. *Scripta Classica Israelica* **14**. 87-110.

Royal Commission on the Ancient and Historical Monuments of Scotland. 1956. *The County of Roxburgh.* Vol. 1. 169-172. Edinburgh.

Royal Commission on the Ancient and Historical Monuments of Scotland. 1997. *Eastern Dumfriesshire: an archaeological landscape.* 179-182. Edinburgh.

Salvatore, J.P. 1996. *Roman Republican Castrametation.* BAR Int. Series **630**.

Schulten, A. 1914-1931. *Numantia. Die Ergebnisse der Ausgrabungen, 1905-1912.* Vols. I-IV. F. Bruckmann, Munich.

Schulten, A. 1933a. Masada: die Burg des Herodes und die römischen Lager. *Zeitschrift des deutschen Palästina-vereins.* **56**, 1-185.

Schulten, A. 1933b. *Geschichte von Numantia.* Piloty & Loehle, Munich.

Shatzman, I. 1991. *The Armies of the Hasmonaeans and Herod.* J.C.B. Mohr (Paul Siebeck), Tübingen.

Stoffel, E.G.H.C. Baron. 1887. *Histoire de Jules César. Guerre Civile.* Imprimerie Nationale, Paris.

Strobel, A. 1974a. Das römische Belagerungswerk um Machärus. *Zeitschrift des deutschen Palästina-vereins.* **90**, 128-184.

Strobel, A. 1974b. Observations about the Roman Installations at Mukawer. *Annual of the Department of Antiquities of Jordan.* **19**, 101-127.

Ussishkin, D. 1978. Excavations at Tel Lachish 1973-1977. Preliminary Report. *Tel Aviv.* **5**, 1-98.

Ussishkin, D. 1980. The 'Lachish Reliefs' and the City of Lachish. *Israel Exploration Journal.* **30**, 175-195.

Ussishkin, D. 1982. *The Conquest of Lachish by Sennacherib.* Tel Aviv University Publications.

Ussishkin, D. 1983. Excavations at Tel Lachish 1978-1983. Second Preliminary Report. *Tel Aviv.* **10**, 97-185.

Ussishkin, D. 1990. The Assyrian Attack on Lachish : the Archaeological Evidence from the Southwest Corner of the Site. *Tel Aviv.* **17**, 53-86.

Ussishkin, D. 1993. Archaeological Soundings at Betar, Bar-Kochba's Last Stronghold. *Tel Aviv.* **20**, 66-97.

Ussishkin, D. 1996. Excavations and Restoration Work at Tel Lachish 1985-1994. Third Preliminary Report. *Tel Aviv.* **23**, 1-60.

Veith, G. 1920. *Der Feldzug von Dyrrhachium zwischen Caesar und Pompejus.* L.W. Seidel & Sohn, Vienna.

Webster, G. 1985. *The Roman Imperial Army.* 3rd Ed. A&C Black, London.

Welfare, H. & Swan, V. 1995. *Roman Camps in England: the field archaeology.* RCHME, London.

Wilson, V. 1974. The Kouklia Sanctuary. *Report of the Department of Antiquities, Cyprus, 1974.* 139-146.

Wimmel, W. 1974. *Die technische Seite von Caesar's Unternehmen gegen Avaricum.* Akademie der Wissenschaften und der Literatur, Mainz.

Yadin, Y. 1963a. *The Art of Warfare in Biblical Lands.* Weidenfeld & Nicolson, London.

Yadin, Y. 1963b. *The Finds from the Bar Kokhba Period in the Cave of Letters.* Israel Exploration Fund, Jerusalem.

Yadin, Y. 1971. *Bar Kokhba.* Weidenfeld & Nicholson, London.

Yadin, Y. & Netzer, E. 1993. Masada. In: Stern, E., Lewinson-Gilboa, A. & Aviram, J. (eds) *The New Encyclopedia of Archaeological Excavations in the Holy Land.* **3**, 973-985. Simon & Schuster, New York.

Zertal, A. 1995. The Roman siege-system at Khirbet el-Hamam (Narbata). In: *The Roman and Byzantine Near East: Some Recent Archaeological Research.* Journal of Roman Studies Supplementary Series **14**, 70-94. Ann Arbor.

INDEX

If you are interested in purchasing other books published by Tempus,
or in case you have difficulty finding any Tempus books in your local bookshop,
you can also place orders directly through our website

www.tempus-publishing.com